Easy Geocaching

Simple Cache Containers

Vince Migliore

January, 2017

Blossom Hill Books

Title ID Number: 6810463
Title: **Easy Geocaching:Simple Cache Containers**

Description: **Easy Geocaching: Simple Cache Containers** is a step-by-step guide for getting started in the fun hobby of geocaching. This book includes instructions on building your own geocache containers.

ISBN-13: 978-1541306714

ISBN-10: 1541306716

Primary Category: Sports & Recreation / General
Country of Publication: United States
Language: English
Search Keywords: geocaching, guide, how-to, treasure hunting
Author: Vince Migliore

Blossom Hill Books
113 Sombrero Way
Folsom, California 95630 USA

Reorder: https://www.createspace.com/6810463

First Edition, January 1, 2017

Table of Contents

Acknowledgements

Several people helped with this book, including fellow geocachers Lynjer7 and Linda#1. Mary Pessaran provided editing support and Charlayne Mattingly offered enduring encouragement.

Chapter 1:
What is Geocaching?

Congratulations!

You're about to discover why geocaching is one of the fastest growing hobbies in America! Geocaching combines the fun of treasure hunting with the benefits of outdoor activity and the mental challenge of problem solving. Just where is that cache hidden? Follow the clues, navigate to the cache site, and match your wits against the clever person who hid the prize.

What is geocaching?

Geocaching.com, the most popular website supporting the hobby, defines geocaching as "a real-world outdoor treasure hunting game. Players try to locate hidden containers, called geocaches, using GPS-enabled devices and then share their experiences online."

The three key points are:

- It's a real-world outdoor game. You have to get out to a park or a bike path or some secret location to find the cache.

- You search for a treasure, or geocache (pronounced GEE-oh-cash). The cache itself is usually a small box or container that holds a log book and sometimes trade items, such as toys and trinkets. See **Figure 1**.

- You find the prize by looking in the area referenced by latitude and longitude coordinates. Most people use hand-held geo-positioning satellite (GPS) devices but you might also use internet map sites or smart-phone apps to find the exact location.

Technically, you don't *need* a GPS device because you can look up the coordinates on a mapping site, such as Google Earth, and get quite close to the right location, where the container is hidden. Having a hand-held GPS device, however, makes the search much easier. You can also use smart-phone apps in place of a GPS device, but they are not as accurate.

Figure 1. This is a typical geocache container. The logbook (left) was stuffed into a false branch on a tree.

Why is it so much fun?

There are as many reasons people get hooked on this sport. Some folks like the mental challenge of solving the puzzle of where the cache is hidden. Others like to combine the game with hiking, bicycling, or other outdoor or fitness activities. Youngsters and the young-at-heart love to open the box and see what's inside that they can trade.

Once you get started, however, the hobby becomes more enjoyable; it grows on you! You meet friends; you engage in friendly competition; you start hiding your own caches, and you get involved with the different aspects of geocaching. There are educational Earth Caches, rough terrain caches, difficult to solve puzzles, and a variety of challenges.

How is it played?

The basic procedure for playing is to look at a map of geocaches in your area. You find such maps on the Internet. The prime hobby site is Geocaching.com, where you can enter an address and see all the caches in that neighborhood. The caches are rated by difficulty and terrain. **Difficulty** refers to how hard it is to locate the cache. *Terrain* describes the struggle to navigate the landscape where the cache is hidden. Both scales range from one to five. A terrain at level 1, for example, might be a flat sidewalk, while level 5 might be a rock that requires ropes to scale to the top.

You choose a few nearby caches, download the cache description and coordinates to your GPS device, then start driving or hiking to the cache site. The exact location where it is hidden is called *ground zero*. Once there, it takes some skill and detective work to find the cache.

For example, the coordinates might lead you to a pine tree. The tree has several pine cones hanging from it, but one of them looks like it's made out of plastic. This in fact is the man-made cache container disguised to fit in with its surroundings. The container is hollow and opens up to show the log book. It takes a sharp eye to locate it. The cache can be hidden inside a knothole of a tree, concealed within a fence post, or magnetically attached to the bottom of a metal object. This is where your detective skills come into play.

Sometimes you can get to within 100 feet or so of ground zero and then realize your path is blocked. You may have to back-track and approach it from another angle. Even at ground zero (GZ) you may have difficulty.

Once you find the cache, you open it up and sign the log book. If you find something inside to trade, you replace it with your own donation of equal or greater value. Some people leave a trademark or signature item to show others they've been there. You might also find a travel bug or geocoin. These you can take, but not permanently. They are designed to move from one cache to another. **Figure 2** shows a typical cache container.

Figure 2. This is a typical plastic cache container with a travel bug (left), a geo-coin, and a small folded log book inside a plastic sleeve.

Finally, you close up the cache, replace it as you found it, and then head home to document your conquest. Go back on the internet to the cache website and record the caches you found, or didn't find. The geocaching websites keep a record of the caches you've completed, including their difficulty and terrain ratings.

Chapter 2:
The Trial Run

Read this chapter if you are not sure you want to make a commitment to geocaching. Check out this process of finding a few caches as a trial run. I think you'll be pleasantly surprised at how much fun it is.

In this Trial Run, you will not need to buy a GPS unit or even pay for membership with Geocaching.com.

Even if you are already sold on the idea of geocaching or already have a GPS unit, this chapter is still an excellent way to help you play the game. It adds another gadget to your toolbox to augment your skills.

The No GPS Method

Before you run out and buy an expensive GPS unit, we highly recommend you find your first caches without one. Instead use internet map sites to pinpoint the location of a few caches and use your brain alone to find the prize. Even if you already have a GPS unit, this exercise is well worth the effort, as it provides a back-up method of finding caches that will supplement your searches and improve your ability to find caches even when you have a GPS unit.

This "dry run" method entails copying the cache coordinates from the Geocaching.com website, then pasting them into a map site. You can then zoom in and even use street views to guide you to the correct location.

Sign up with Geocaching.com

Now, let's sign up for your free Geocaching.com account. Go to your computer. Sign on to Geocaching.com.

Click on the FREE Basic account. You can use your Facebook account as an alternative. Take some time to think about what User Name you choose. It will be with you for a long time. Once registered you will receive an email to validate your account.

Note: If you have decided to choose the paid membership, then check out Chapter 4 for a more detailed registration process.

Step-by-Step:
Find caches without a GPS unit

Go again to the home page and select "PLAY." Note: The Geocaching web page changes often, so PLAY might be replace by something similar, such as "Find a Cache." The geocaching.com home page pull-down menus are shown in **Figure 3.**

1. Enter your starting address in the box that appears. Alternatively, you can enter your city or zip code.

2. Click on "Add Filters." You will see **Figure 4**.

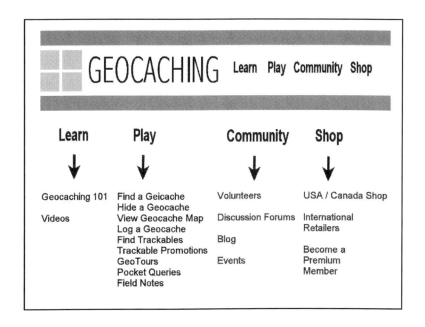

Figure 3. Home page pull-down menus.

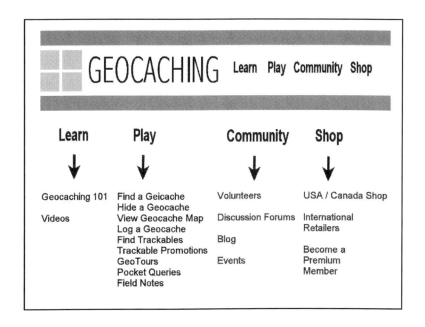

Figure 4. Screen for selected easy caches.

3. Set Difficulty to 2.5. You do this by clicking on the middle of the line.

4. Set Terrain to 2.5 or less.

5. Click on the "Search" box. You will see a page listing nearby caches that should be easy to find. **Figure 5.**

6. Select 3 or 4 candidate caches that are near each other.

7. Click on each one in turn and read the log entries. Be sure they have been found in the last few months. A typical cache page is shown in **Figure 6**.

8. At the top of the page for each cache that has been found lately, copy the coordinates.

9. Paste the coordinates into an internet map site, such as Google Maps.

10. Zoom in on the location making a note of the surroundings, how to get there, and any landmarks you can use to locate the cache once you are at the site.

11. Many map sites, including Google Earth allow you to view the area from eye level street view. Look at the area from the street

view, again noting any landmarks or clues that you can use to locate the cache.

12. Take notes where you think the cache might be hidden. If there is nothing but a tree or a park bench at the site, that is most likely your search area. Write out or copy and mark a map of where you will be going.

13. Go to the site and look for the cache.

14. If you find it, open it up and sign the log book, then return it as found.

15. If you have not found any of them, go back online and navigate to Geocaching.com.

16. Click on your user name and log in. You will see the recently viewed cache listings at the top.

17. Record your finds, or did-not-finds (DNFs).

18. Voila! You've done it without a GPS.

My Lists

Geocache Name	Distance	Favorites	Size	Difficulty	Terrain	Last Found	Placed on
Century Marker TeamWalkers	0.5 mi W	5	Small	1.5	2.5	12/29/2016	01/14/2017
Scout Cache #7 Scout Troop 44	0.7 mi SE	4	Small	1.5	1.5	11/19/2016	04/01/2016
Blue Lizzie DogBoy	0.9 mi N	1	Micro	2.5	2.5	10/11/2016	09/10/2014
Lamp Post 3 Shelby Family	1.1 mi NW	11	Other	1.5	1.5	12/12/2016	12/30/2015
White Rock Rock Boy	1.2 mi N	2	Medium	3.5	3.0	07/21/2015	02/14/2011

Figure 5. Screen for selected easy caches.

This method is useful even when you do have a GPS. Many geocachers look up the locations on map sites for several reasons:

- Internet maps help you find the cache.

- The map shows the type of terrain allowing you to prepare properly.

- If there are lots of trees in the area, the cache might be a "hanger" and you will need a pole to retrieve it.

- Internet maps help you find a place to park, especially for off-road locations, such as parks and bike trails.

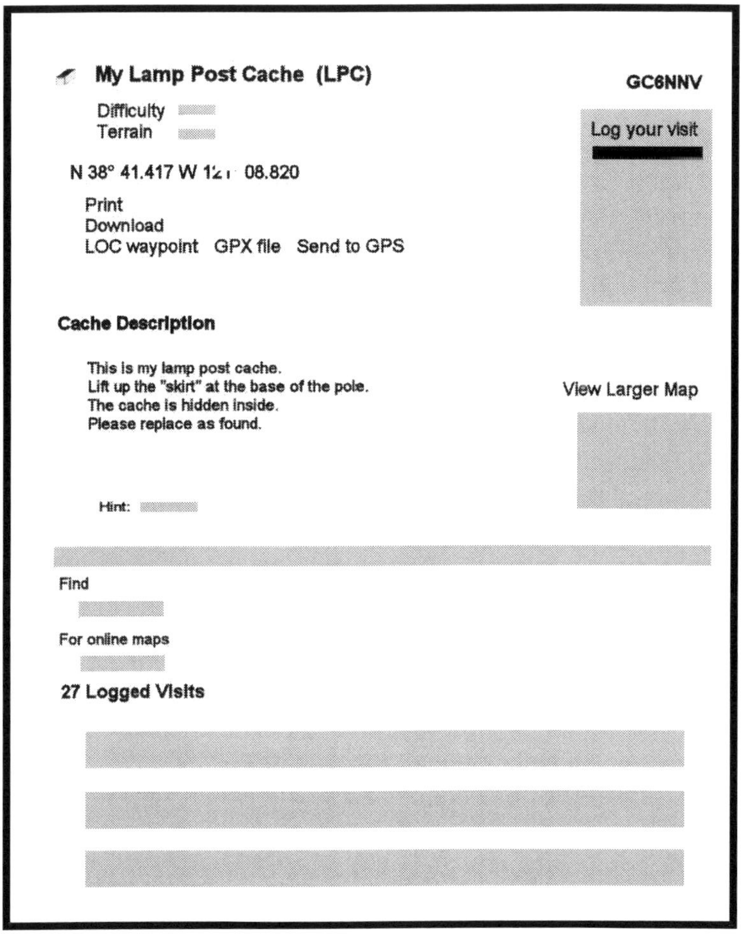

My Lamp Post Cache (LPC)   **GC6NNV**

Difficulty
Terrain   Log your visit

N 38° 41.417 W 121 08.820

Print
Download
LOC waypoint   GPX file   Send to GPS

Cache Description

This is my lamp post cache.
Lift up the "skirt" at the base of the pole.   View Larger Map
The cache is hidden inside.
Please replace as found.

Hint:

Find

For online maps

27 Logged Visits

Figure 6. Typical geocache listing.

16

Chapter 3:
Learn the Language

In order to play the game of geocaching you need to learn some of the language. These terms are fun and easy. You may have picked up a few already from **Chapter 1**. These words evolved from the long history of geocaching.

Most important terms

The most important words to learn are summarized here. A longer list follows.

It's best if you become familiar with these most common words and then look up the others later when you come across them.

A **geocache**, or cache, is the name used for the container or the exact location where it is hidden. A geocacher is a person who is looking for the hidden containers. Sometimes the geocacher is called a cacher for short. You might say "The geocacher hid his cache inside a hollow log.

Geocaching refers to the entire hobby of looking for caches. Geocaching, the verb, can also mean you are going out to look for some caches. People who know nothing about geocaching are called **muggles**. The Harry Potter books refer to muggles as ordinary people or non-wizards. The terms have been adopted by the geocaching community. "I'm going out geocaching with two other cachers. We are taking along a muggle to show him how it works."

Sometimes people find a hidden cache by accident. Occasionally they will remove or empty out the container, not knowing that it's part of a game. This is what you call being muggled. "I hid a geochache but it got muggled."

Coordinates are the latitude and longitude that describe where the geocache is located. Latitude and longitude are used in mapping and navigating to pinpoint an exact spot on the earth. That spot is called **ground zero**, or GZ, in geocaching. There are different ways of writing coordinates. The format used in geocaching is Degrees and Minutes with three decimals for minutes.
Example: N 38 41.500, W 121 08.333.

If a cache is hidden in a grassy field and several people have already found it, they may have trampled the grass so much that you can see exactly where they walked. This tell-tale marking on the ground is called a **geotrail**. "I found the cache easily. The geotrail led me right to ground zero!" See **Figure 6**.

Glossary

Archive: To discontinue a cache. It is removed from the Geocaching.com website.

Attribute: A pre-defined description of conditions surrounding a cache. Attributes use little pictures, or icons, on the cache web page to tell you what to expect. It includes such things as whether there is parking nearby, or if it is accessible by wheelchair. There are icons for hazards too, such as poison oak or ticks in the area. The Geocaching.com website has a complete description at: http://www.geocaching.com/about/glossary.aspx.

BYOP: Bring your own pen. Many caches are too small to hold a writing implement. If you want to sign the log you will have to bring your own pen.

Cache: This is the same as Geocache; a container holding a logbook and possibly other items.

Cacher: A person who engages in geocaching.

CITO: Cache In, Trash Out. This is an operating principle for all geocachers. If you find a cache that has trash around it, make a genuine attempt to clean it up. Some events have that clean-up process as the main focus of the cache, so that participants will bring trash bags for a major clean-up. A CITO event is also a type of activity where participants include environmental clean-up as part of the cache adventure.

D/T: Difficulty and Terrain. Geocaching.com rates caches on the overall difficulty of finding the cache, on a 1 to 5 scale, and the terrain, from flat ground to mountain climbing, or where special equipment needed. A cache that is in plain sight might be rated difficulty 1, while a hollowed out pine cone on a tree full of pine cones might rate a 4 in difficulty. A bike path, where you can walk right up to the cache might have a terrain rating of 1, but one where you need a canoe to reach an island would be rated 5 difficulty.

Difficulty: See D/T. This is the overall difficulty of finding the cache.

DNF: Short for Did Not Find. When you fail to find the cache you can log a DNF on the cache web page.

EarthCache: An EarthCache is one that has a geologic, scientific or environmentally significant story to tell you about the Earth. Generally there is no physical cache or log book to sign. Instead, you send answers for specific questions to the cache owner in order to qualify to log the cache. A meteor crater is a good example of an EarthCache. You might find a plaque or poster that describes the area. Questions for such a cache would be "When do scientist think this meteor struck the earth," or "How much did the meteor weigh?" You need to answer these questions correctly to qualify for logging the cache.

Event Cache: A one-time meeting of geocachers. Cache events often have a theme, such as a holiday celebration or a costume party. The event sign-in sheet becomes the log and the cache is archived right after the meeting.

First-to-Find: This is a prize – the honor of saying you were the first one to find a cache when it was newly listed. If you are the first geocacher to locate the cache you will find a blank log and you will get the FTF "honors." Some geocachers are competitive and strive to be the first to find a cache. On occasion, the cache owner will leave a specific prize for the FTF person.

FTF: See First-to-Find.

GC code: Geocaching.com assigns a unique code number to each listed cache. The code number appears in the upper right corner of each cache web page. Geocaching.com codes begin with GC; example, GC4F81V is one of the author's cache code numbers.

Geocache: The geocache is a container that holds a log book which you sign when you find it. It may contain toys and trinkets (called SWAG), or trading items, such as travel bugs and signature items.

Geocacher: A person who is engaged in geocaching.

Figure 7. A typical "geotrail" where the grass is trampled leading up the hill to the cache site.

Geocoin: A coin or emblem that is traded by placing it in the geocache. The geocoin is numbered and tracked on geocaching sites. The owner of the geocoin can look up where it has traveled and who has moved it.

Geotrail: A marking on the grass or earth which shows that human traffic has passed by and may indicate the cache location. See **Figure 7**.

GPS: Global-Positioning Satellite. GPS is a hand-held or automobile based device that uses satellite signals to determine your current latitude and longitude.

GPX: A data file containing all or most of the information describing a geocache. It is downloaded from a web page and stored on your GPS device.

Ground Zero: The exact location, defined by latitude and longitude, where the cache can be found.

GZ: See Ground Zero.

Latitude, Longitude: Latitude and longitude are the imaginary lines that crisscross the globe and make it easier for people and ships to navigate to a specific location. There are different ways to write these numbers but for geocaching the most common form is to use degrees and minutes with three decimal places for the minutes, such as N 40° 46.152 W 073° 58.689. This is the standard format for geocachers. The same location can be written with degrees, minutes, and seconds, and it takes the form: N 40° 46' 09.120" W 73° 58' 41.340".

Letterbox. A Letterbox is a variation on the traditional geocache. It was a sport invented before the use of the GPS system and employs a description, a map, or a puzzle that has to be solved in order to find the treasure. It has now been incorporated into the broader-based geocaching hobby. The Letterbox contains a log book and a rubber stamp with a stamp pad. Letterbox players carry their own stamp and log book to the location. They use their own personal stamp to leave an impression on the cache logbook, as well as using the Letterbox stamp to mark their own personal log book. This way, both the Letterbox owner and the Letterbox players collect impressions of each other's stamps.

LPC: An abbreviation for the log: Lamp Post Cache. Most lamp posts have a metal skirt around the base to cover the retaining bolts. This cover can lift up and provides a common hiding place for a cache.

Multi-cache: A two-part or multi-stage geocache puzzle. You might use your GPS device to navigate to the first stage, where you will find further instructions or coordinates to direct you to another location.

Mystery cache: A mystery cache, or puzzle cache, is a form of geocaching where you have to solve a puzzle or riddle to find the final location. An example is to

24

provide starting coordinates then ask the player to answer questions. Example: What year was President Obama born? Add the last two digits of that year to the North coordinates and subtract it from the West coordinates. The revised coordinates indicate the final Ground Zero. Puzzle caches can get quite difficult, but they provide a unique challenge.

Offset cache: See Multi-Cache

Puzzle cache: See Mystery cache.

Signature item: A signature item is something with your name, or more often your geocaching name, that you leave inside a cache to show you were there. People often make up their own signature items, such as a wooden nickel disk with their name stamped on it, or a hand-painted rock. Some people buy special-purpose signature items such as small metal coins, business cards, or personalized stickers that they leave in the cache.

SL: Signed Log: an abbreviation used when logging your visit on the cache web page log.

Spoiler: A photo or description that gives away the location of the cache. If a cache is hidden behind a loose brick in a wall, the spoiler might say "Third brick from the end, six rows up." A spoiler will destroy the challenge of finding the cache, but sometimes the searcher is in a hurry.

SWAG: Stuff We All Get. This is a term derived from the donations that celebrities get for attending public events. For geocaching it translates into the toys, trinkets and (well, let's be honest) "junk" that people leave for trade or give-away in the cache container.

Terrain: or Terrain Rating: This is the level of difficulty, 1 to 5, for the pathway or conditions for getting to the cache. A sidewalk on level ground would be a terrain rating of 1. If special equipment is required, such as a ladder or a rope, the Terrain Rating would be higher, such as 3.5. The most difficult caches, where you need mountain gear or a boat, will go as high as 5 on the difficulty scale.

TFTC: Abbreviation for the log: "Thanks for the cache."

TNLN: Took nothing, left nothing. Some cache containers are large enough to allow trading trinkets and toys. Geocaching etiquette suggests that if you take an item from the cache then you should leave one of equal or greater value.

TOTT: Abbreviation for cache description: "Tricks of the trade," or "Tools of the trade." This usually refers to a long stick you may need to retrieve a cache from a high spot. Tools of the trade are common items used to help you find or retrieve the cache. This includes sticks with a magnet or hook on the end, a mirror, a compass, a telescoping pole, or a set of tweezers to remove the log from a tight container. Example: Many metal fence posts have a rounded cap on top. Experienced cachers like to glue a box or film canister inside the removable cap. This is a trick of the trade.

Traditional Cache: This is the normal cache described by coordinates and it's the one and only location. There are no puzzles to solve or stages to go through.

Travel Bug: Travel bugs are toys, figurines, coins, or emblems that have a tag with a tracking number so the owner can follow where the bug has been. The travel bug is not kept by the geocacher, but is instead transported to another cache. It can travel all over the world.

UPR: An abbreviation for the log: "Unusual Pile of Rocks." This is given as a clue or spoiler for others to help find the cache.

Virtual Cache: A cache that does not have a log book to sign or a container to find. A statue of George Washington might serve as a virtual cache. In order to verify that you found it you would have to send information to the cache owner proving you were there. This is generally a set of questions that you can answer by visiting the virtual cache. Example: What year was the statue placed there? Who was the sculptor?

Chapter 4:
Buying a GPS Device

There are several different GPS devices that you can use to find caches. Each of them has their advantages and disadvantages. You also have the option of not buying a GPS device and continue searching using the online maps and paper notes that we've covered in Chapter 2. If you do decide you want to buy a device there are many routes and techniques. These are:

1. GPS app on a smart phone or tablet.

2. Automobile GPS in a car.

3. Low-end hand-held devices

4. High-end (paperless) hand-held devices

Let's look at each of these options.

GPS app on a smart phone or tablet

Smart phones, tablets, and an increasing number of hand-held devices allow you to download programs, called applications, or apps, which enable you to mimic the workings of a hand-held GPS device. These are available for iPhone and Android devices. Enter "geocaching GPS apps" on any search engine online and you will see a long list of such programs. An app called "Geocaching" by Geocaching.com is available, for example, from iTunes at low cost. Likewise, Google Play offers several geocaching apps. The names, capabilities and costs of these programs change all the time, so it requires a web search to stay current.

The advantages of using a smart phone or portable device is that it's a quick and relatively simple way to get into the geocaching game – that is IF you already have a smart phone.

The disadvantages: The costs of using phone data programs where you are in effect surfing the internet as you search, can be pretty expensive. Another problem is that phone applications are not as accurate as a device that is made specifically for geocaching.

Dedicated GPS devices can link to several satellites at once so that the technology is much more accurate at pin-pointing your location. They have a very sensitive antenna built in, so they are far superior to the phone applications. In addition, they are designed to draw less power than a cell phone.

If you decide to use a smart phone, then you would start by looking at which programs are available for your phone or tablet. Use a search engine to find "Android geocaching apps" for example if you have an Android device, or iTunes if you have an iPhone.

Automobile GPS devices

Only SOME of the GPS units that are made for cars and trucks will work with the files you get from Geocaching.com. Some of the more expensive and advanced models allow you to download geocache locations to the car device. These are very handy if you are driving to most of your caches, but you would need the kind of unit that detaches from the car so you can carry it along a path or bike trail. For this reason it may be better to consider a hand-held GPS device that is made specifically for geocaching.

Low-cost hand-held devices

There are two broad categories of GPS devices that are made for geocaching, the low cost kind, and the high end or paperless kind.

Low-cost units give you much of what you need for a fun adventure. There is still a lot of preparation necessary. You have to write things down, such as where the cache is located and its difficulty rating. When you have a GPS unit, this information is loaded into the memory of the GPS and you can see the basic description and notes.

Even with this data, there are oftentimes things you still have to write down such as the hints in logs written by previous visitors. The low-cost units provide you with all the basic information, such as the coordinates, the difficulty, and when it was last found. The more expensive paperless devices cost a lot more, but they hold a larger volume of the information that you see on the cache page. The file downloaded to this type of unit includes all the logs of previous visitors, which can help in finding the cache.

The Big Four manufactures for hand-held GPS units are Delorme, Garmin, Lowrance, and Magellan, in alphabetical order. Reviews of their products can be found on the Geocaching.com website. You can also find reviews on shopping and auction sites, such as Amazon.com.

Some examples of entry-level geocaching units:

- Garmin eTrex 10: This costs about $100.

- Magellan eXplorist 110: About $120.

- Magellan eXplorist GC: About $130.

Examples of hand-held GPS devices are shown in
Figure 8. There is also a low-cost device called the
Geomate Jr., made for youngsters. It sells for under
$100 and comes with geocaches pre-loaded on the
device.

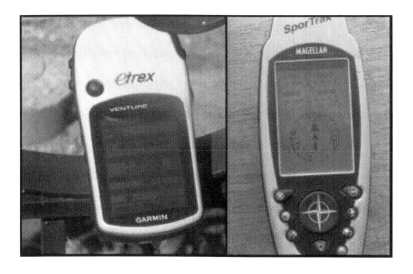

Figure 8. GPS devices for geocaching will fit in the
palm of your hand.

High-end (paperless) hand-held devices

The more expensive GPS units generally cost over $200, so buying one is a big decision. If you're a beginner, it's probably best to wait until you know a lot more about what features are important before you make such an investment.

The big advantage of the more expensive models is that they can hold just about all the information on a cache that you can see on the cache's web page. This includes its location, the full description, previous log entries, and the hint, if there is one. Photographs are usually NOT included in the file that is transferred to the GPS unit. A large memory allows you to download hundreds of caches in your area all at once.

The features to consider are:

- Pre-loaded maps and software.

- The amount of memory it has.

- Pocket Queries – the ability to download many cache files at once.

- Ruggedness, including waterproofing.

A thorough discussion of buying a GPS unit is also found at the geocaching.com website.

Chapter 5:
After You Buy a GPS

Inspection

Congratulations on getting your GPS unit! Most units will need a battery and a memory card which are not always included. There are three things you have to do:

- Read the Instruction Manual.

- Read the Instruction Manual.

- Read the Instruction Manual.

No, that's not a typo, though it may be a bit of tongue-in-cheek teasing. Read the manual once through quickly to see the important areas of information. Read it again more thoroughly to be sure you understand everything. Finally, read it again focusing on areas that you have difficulty understanding.

If you are going geocaching with friends, many of them may be able to guide you on how and when to use your GPS features.

Transfer software

No one tells you this, but the GPS is like a little mini-computer. It requires specific software, often pre-installed, in order to operate properly. The software allows your computer to talk with the GPS unit. The software transfers the geocache files to your GPS device. Each manufacturer has its own dedicated program.

For example, the Garmin software download is at: http://software.garmin.com/en-US/gcp.html.

For Magellan: http://support.magellangps.com/support/index.php.

There are also third-party programs that work with multiple manufacturers.
See: http://www.easygps.com/, for Garmin, Magellan, and Lowrance.

The Geocaching website has a page which discusses different types of GPS software.
See: http://www.geocaching.com/software/.

These programs work automatically when you plug your GPS into the computer. You are now ready to download geocaching information, called GPX files, to your GPS.

- Most such programs will open up a window on your computer automatically once you plug the GPS cable in to the USB port. If that doesn't work with yours, then navigate to the program location and double click on it.

- Next, open a web browser to the Geocaching.com web page.

- Log in to Geocaching.com

- Click on the third tab **PLAY** menu and select **Find a geocACHE**.

- Enter a street address or ZIP code for you starting point.

- In the upper right corner, click on "Map the first 1,000 caches. This shows caches on a map.

Loading caches

On the map page a diagram appears on your computer showing the many caches in your area. **Figure 9** is a typical example.

The idea today is to select 4 or 5 caches that are relatively near each other, and near your house, so you can make an afternoon adventure of geocaching.

Geocache Name	Distance	Favorites	Size	Difficulty	Terrain	Last Found	Placed on
My Lists							
Century Marker TeamWalkers	0.5 mi W	5	Small	1.5	2.5	12/29/2016	01/14/2017
Scout Cache #7 Scout Troop 44	0.7 mi SE	4	Small	1.5	1.5	11/19/2016	04/01/2016
Blue Lizzie DogBoy	0.9 mi N	1	Micro	2.5	2.5	10/11/2016	09/10/2014
Lamp Post 3 Shelby Family	1.1 mi NW	11	Other	1.5	1.5	12/12/2016	12/30/2015
White Rock Rock Boy	1.2 mi N	2	Medium	3.5	3.0	07/21/2015	02/14/2011

Figure 9. This is a page of cache listings. The Difficulty and Terrain (D/T) and the cache size are listed in columns 5 and 6.

Step-by-Step:
Loading GPS files

1. Connect your GPS to your computer using the USB cable. The computer should recognize your GPS device as described above.

2. Sign on to Geocaching.com. Click on the Play tab at the top and select Find a Cache.

3. Enter your street address or the address where you want to start looking for caches.

4. You will see a LIST of nearby caches. At the top right of the page, click on MAP, or Map the first 1000 caches.

5. Look around the map of your area. Zoom in for a closer look if necessary. See if there is a park, a school yard, or a bike path that has several caches near each other. You may have to move the map around by clicking and dragging the mouse pointer.

6. As an example, let's say there are four caches along a trail in a nearby park. For each of the four caches .

a. Click on the cache and look at the last date it was found. If it hasn't been found recently this is a sign of trouble. You may have to ignore it. The date of the last find is in the upper right corner of the most recent log entry.

b. Likewise, if the last few logs show DNF (Did Not Find) that is an indication that you will not have success with this cache. Avoid caches that show **NEEDS MAINTENANCE**. These will have a little red wrench icon showing in the cache description.

c. Look at the difficulty and terrain ratings. Select this cache for your adventure only if you feel reasonably comfortable with the difficulty ratings. Beginners should choose a rating of 2.5 or lower.

d. Look at the size of the cache. Larger caches are generally easier to find.

e. Look at the number of favorite points the cache has. This is a good sign of an enjoyable adventure.

f. Click on the **VIEW LARGER MAP** link at the lower right map. Zoom in closer to view the cache and select **SATELLITE** view in the upper right corner. This will give you an idea of the terrain and surrounding. You will see a map similar to **Figure 10**.

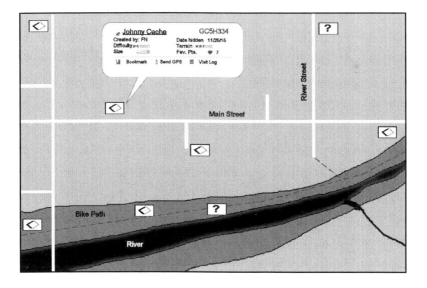

Figure 10. Map view of cache listings.

41

7. From the map view you can look at the details of the cache page by clicking on any cache title. See **Figure 11**.

8. For each of the caches you are interested in, click on the **SEND TO MY GPS** box near the top. This transfers the cache file from the web page to your GPS. There is a **Send to** box for the GPX file on both the group listing page and the individual cache pages.

9. Once you have completed these steps you should have a few caches that are relatively close and for which you feel reasonably comfortable. This is what we call your geocaching **route**.

10. It's best to select about 5 caches in a row and expect that one or two of them might not be found. Send each of them to your GPS as described above.

11. You may want to consider zooming in and out on the map so that it shows the caches you have selected, and then you can print the map off your computer. This will serve as a guide once you're out in the field. Write the cache name on the printout, as well as any hints or pointers you gathered from studying the cache description.

This procedure is the first of many route plans you will be creating in your geocaching career. If you are working with a group of geocachers they often trade turns in creating the geocaching route.

The next step is to go out into the field and search for the caches. Before your field trip, however, decide if you want to go it alone or with a partner or two.

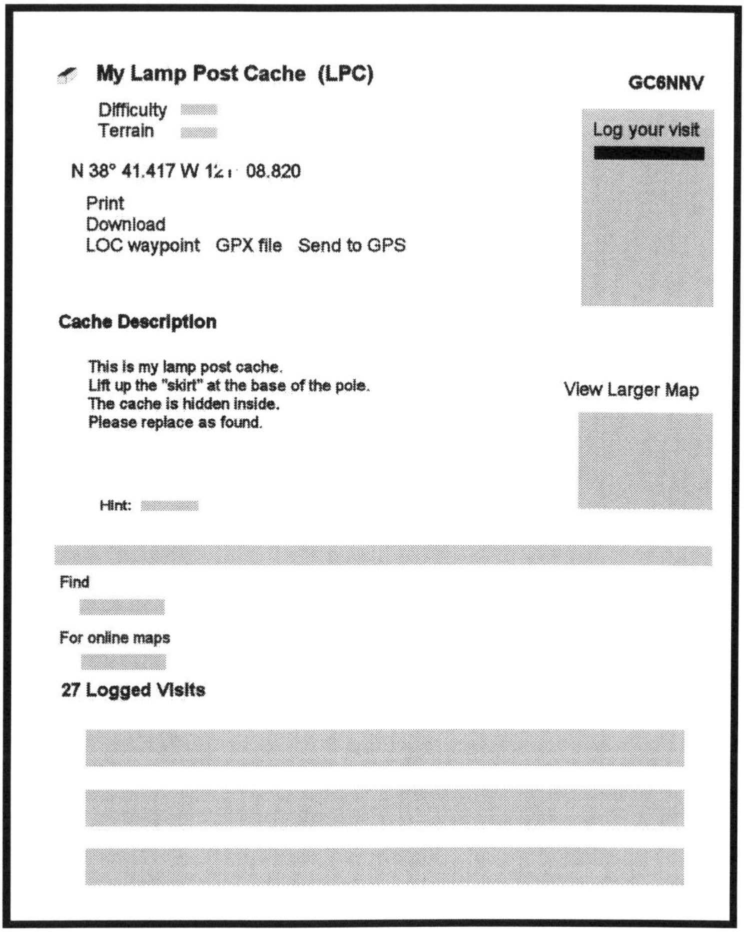

My Lamp Post Cache (LPC)

GC6NNV

Difficulty
Terrain

Log your visit

N 38° 41.417 W 121 08.820

Print
Download
LOC waypoint   GPX file   Send to GPS

Cache Description

This is my lamp post cache.
Lift up the "skirt" at the base of the pole.
The cache is hidden inside.
Please replace as found.

View Larger Map

Hint:

Find

For online maps

27 Logged Visits

Figure 11. This is a typical cache detail page Use this page to view cache description and details, to read the logs and to send GPX files to your GPS unit. Use this page to log your visits.

44

Chapter 6:
Go With a Friend

You are just about ready for your field trip. There is just one more matter to consider:
- Do you want to go alone or with a friend?

Going with a friend is generally much better. The hobby of geocaching is more enjoyable when you can share experiences with a friend. There are also some practical benefits. Two sets of eyes can find the cache much faster. Moreover, two people together are safer than one person alone.

Going with another newbie

A Newbie, or newcomer to the sport, is someone not yet familiar with the game. The advantage of taking a current friend or family member is that you know each other already, and you might both be interested in learning the game together. When two or more people work together, things just seem to go more smoothly. One person might be better at the computer work described in the previous chapters while another might be better at outdoor activities.

Going with an experienced geocacher

It's surprisingly easy to find another geocacher to go out with for your first run. It's important to set aside any shyness you might have because 99% or geocachers are thrilled and honored to be asked by someone to help with their first adventure. Going with another geocacher (**Figure 12**) offers an opportunity to learn from their experience, and another set of eyes makes finding the cache a lot faster.

CAUTION: Use common sense and good judgment if you decide to go geocaching with someone you don't know very well. While problems are extremely rare, it's best if you have all their contact information and let others know when you expect to go and return.

.

Figure 12. Going with another geocacher makes the trip more fun and provides another set of eyes to help find the cache.

Step-by-Step:
Linking up with another geocacher

1. Go back to **Step-by-Step: Loading GPX fines** (page 39) and repeat steps 1 through 4 to see a list of caches in your area.

2. Click on caches near your home and look at the log listings. For each listing, look at the names of the people who have made log entries.

3. As you go through the cache logs for the different listings you'll see many of the same names popping up for each cache. These are your neighbor cachers.

4. Look for names that indicate a family or team, such as "TeamWilson" or "The KatzFamily."

5. Click on the name in blue letters on the left side of their log entry. This brings you to their Profile Page

6. Look at their gallery – you may find pictures of people you can feel comfortable with. The

GALLERY can be found on the 5th tab across the top of their profile page.

7. If you find someone who might be a good instructor, click on the Send Email, or Send Message link on the left side of the page.

8. In your message tell them what you're interested in; a little guidance in finding your first cache. The message might go something like this. "Hello neighbor. I am new to geocaching and I'm about to go out for my first cache. I see that you have experience in finding caches in this neighborhood. I wonder if I could tag along the next time you go? Better yet, I am looking to find cache XYZ. Maybe you could help me, or know someone who can help. Thank you in advance."

9. Then wait for the reply. It might take a day or two. If they cannot help they will often suggest someone who is more attuned to your needs.

Of course, the experienced geocacher might suggest some changes to your plan. This is a matter for you to negotiate before your outing.

Important: Linking up with other, more experienced, geocachers may alter your plans considerably. The other geocachers may well want to engage in more advanced or rigorous activities, such as more difficult geocache challenges. Going with more advanced players will certainly speed up your learning process, but you have to weigh that against your own level of comfort. Do not be afraid to decline an offer. For example, if they are going on an all-day hike while you are looking for an easy one-hour adventure, then the goals of that group and your needs might not be a good match when you're first starting out.

Chapter 7:
Your First Field Trip

Are you ready for you first field trip? It's a good idea to read through this entire chapter before you go out.

At this point you should have:

- The notes taken for each cache you plan to visit. This includes a map, the hints for finding the cache, and your mental images gained from studying the map aerial views.

- Someone to go with, or a plan to go by yourself.

- Sturdy outdoor clothing with good leg and foot protection.

- The necessary supplies for logging the cache and trading swag items. (See below.)

Remember to let someone know where you are going and when you expect to be back.

What you need to bring

You should now have your papers for each cache. You should have a mental image of where they are located. Now you need to prepare physically for the first cache adventure. See **Figure 13**.

Things you will definitely need:

- Pen, pencil or other writing implement – so you can fill out the log.

- Good walking shoes and leg protection. You may have to squeeze behind a scratchy bush or walk through weeds, so don't wear sandals. Long pants will prevent scratches.

- A pair of tweezers. Some cache logs are tiny and may be hard to extract from the cache.

You may also want to bring small piece of paper if the log book is full.

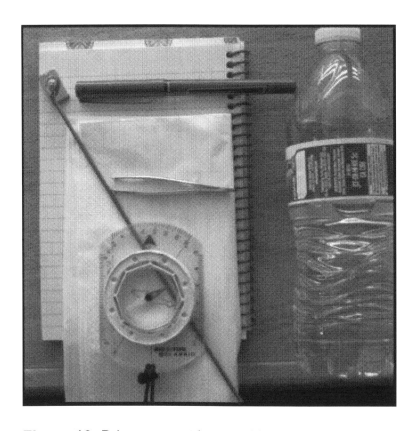

Figure 13. Bring support items with you, such as print-outs of cache details. A few good things to bring are a pen and notebook, paper towels, tweezers, a compass, a probe with a magnet on the end, and water.

Things you might need:

- Small gifts or toys. This is necessary only if you intend to trade swag items if there are any inside the cache. See **Figure 14**.

- A local map.

- A compass.

- A cell phone.

- Water, both for drinking and cleaning your hands. Paper towels.

- Bug spray.

OK! If you've done everything in sequence up to this point you are ready for your first field trip. Nice job! Now you can walk, ride, or drive to the first cache site.

Figure 14. If you like the treasure hunting part of geocaching, bring items to trade or donate.

55

At the cache site

Once you're at the cache site look around for good hiding places. If you were going to hide a little box around here somewhere, where would you put it? Refer now to your notes and the landmarks you saw in the map aerial view. Was there a pole nearby? Did the hint indicate the cache was in a tree? If the description is for a Lamp Post Cache, see if there is a pole around. The base cover of the pole, the skirt, may lift up to reveal the cache. If the cache is a **hanger** then look for a little box or cartridge hanging from the branches of the tree. If the description indicates "magnetic" then look for any metal objects it may be attached to. **Figure 15** shows what some of the typical cache containers look like.

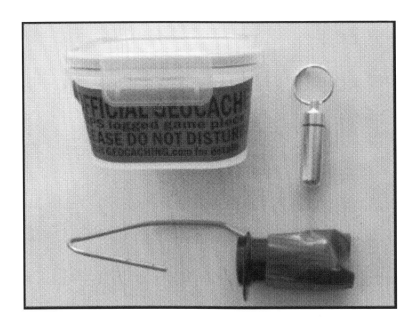

Figure 15. Typical cache containers include a sealed plastic food container, a bison tube, and film canister "hanger."

This is the fun part. You have to use your brain, your detective skills, and logic to discover the hiding spot.

The GPS satellite locating technology is only accurate to about 10 feet, so expand your search area. Put a rock or a mark on the ground where you think Ground Zero is, then walk around in a circle about 10 feet wide to find other possible hiding spots. Remember to look high and low. Geocaching rules require that you cannot bury a cache, so no digging should be involved, but the cache may be hidden by a rock, a log, or a camouflaged cover.

Still can't find it? Here are some Tricks of the Trade:

- Look at the caps on any fence posts. These might lift up to reveal a cache inside.

- Look at unusual rocks. Sometime the Cache Owner will drill a hole in a rock and hide things inside.

- Look for any metal objects; the cache might be stuck magnetically to the metal.

- Look inside tree branches. Many times the cache will have green tape on it.

- Look in knotholes in the tree or cracks in the wood of a telephone pole. Some caches are made of tape and slotted into the crack like a tiny envelope.

- Look for unusual signs or switch-plates. Sometimes a sign is not real and pulls off just like a magnet, and the cache is on the back of the phony sign.

- Look for loose wire hooks or strings. Very often the cache is hidden inside a pole or down a pipe and you have to pull on the string to retrieve it.

- If the cache is in a field, look for trampled grass or a well-worn path. The previous geocachers may have left a trail.

If you and your partners still cannot find it, then stop and take a breath. Give it just one more quick mini-search. This happens only rarely, but it's usually just a matter of experience.

Do not spend so much time that you get frustrated. If two people cannot find the cache in about 20 minutes then do not be afraid to give it up for the time being. Remember, the object is to have fun, and you are just beginning, so let's try another one.

You should have a few other cache sites on your list that you can search. Go to the next one and start over. If you go through all your cache listings and cannot find one, then you always have the opportunity go back onto the computer, look up the cache description again, and write to the Cache Owner, or other geocachers, to give you a hint. They will generally provide some clues that will help you.

Yes! You found your first one! Congratulations!

OK, follow these steps:

- Before you open it up, stop for a second and memorize where it was hidden. You want to be able to put it back in exactly the same place when you are done. If there was a rock covering it, for example, make sure you don't throw the rock away.

- Look around. Make sure that no muggles are watching you.

- Examine the container. Does it have a screw cap? How do you open it?

- Open the container carefully. Sometimes it may have water or bugs inside if it was not sealed well.

- See what's inside. This is the fun part.

- Find the log book. This will be a folded or rolled up sheet of paper with the signatures of previous geocachers. Sometimes, for smaller caches, you may need a tweezers to extract the logbook from a tiny tube.

- See if there are any travel bugs, swag, trade items, toys or notes inside. If you have brought along your own trade items you can exchange one of yours, of about equal value, for one in the cache.

- If you see a travel bug and you want to help move it along, then you can take that too. Write down the travel bug tracking code.

- Sign the log. Use your geocaching name. You will see that most people write the date and their geocaching name. If the log book has plenty of space some people will write a quick Thank You or a smiley face just for the fun of it.

- Make a note to yourself describing what you found. If the log book is wet or there is dirt inside, you may want to enter that into your comments when you log the cache on the computer. If the cache is in an area with a nice view or if you find a well designed cache container, these are things you will want to write about when you make your report on the computer.

- If you have any of your own travel bugs, gifts, or swag that you want to leave then drop it in now. Do not put in anything so bulky that it will prevent you from closing up the cache again.

- Be sure the cache is sealed and return it to its original hiding spot.

- Be a good citizen and take out any trash that might be in the area.

- Review your notes one more time.

- Check your hands and clothing to remove any leaves, debris, or creepy-crawlies that may have landed on you.

- Head back home or to the next cache.

Nice job! Now you will head back home and record your finds, or Did-Not-Finds, on the cache web pages.

Make sure you get back home safe and sound.

Oops! Still can't find it!

Here are some simple steps to review if you cannot find the cache:

- Read the Hint and previous logs for clues on finding the cache.

- Expand your search area

- Look high and low.

- Walk about 15 feet away from ground zero and walk north and south, keeping your eye on the GPS. This arrow will point in the direction of the cache. Do this 3 or 4 times walking in the north-south route to pinpoint the spot where the cache is exactly perpendicular to your route. Do the same thing in the east-west direction. This will help you pinpoint ground zero.

- Read the cache description for hints. If the cache is named "Red Rock" - - well, duh! Look for a red rock. If it's named "Plumbers Playtime," look for a false pipe or valve.

If a reasonable search fails to bring you success, don't spend a lot of time in futile searching. Go to the next cache. When you get back home you can write a message to the cache owner or previous people who found it for a clue.

Chapter 8:
Report Your Finds

Logging your finds

Logging your geocaching adventures creates a
permanent record of your finds, and your attempts.
Even caches that you were not able to find should be
logged. Geocaching.com stores your statistics and
keeps track of how many caches you have found. The
website also tracks what kinds of caches they are,
such as traditional caches or events you've attended.

On your first outing, you probably have a list of the
caches you attempted to find. Now it's time to go back
and record the results of your search. By logging all
your finds and DNFs you can track your progress as
you grow into the sport. You will find that you have
more success at finding caches as you gain
experience.

You may also find that going with a group increases your success rate.

Step-by-Step:
Logging your finds and Did-Not-Finds

1. Navigate to Geocaching.com.

2. If you're not automatically logged in, then click on the **SIGN IN** box at the upper right side of the screen.

3. Click on the **KEEP ME SIGNED IN** box just below the Password box if you want to stay logged in.

4. There a several ways to view the caches that you were looking for. The simplest way may be to select the second tab at the top which reads **YOUR PROFILE**.

5. Move your cursor over the **YOUR PROFILE** tab and click on **QUICK VIEW**.

6. You should see a list of the caches that you were considering, so you can click on the ones

you want to make entries for.

7. If you don't see the cache name that you want to log, then go back to Geocaching.com, the main page and hover over the **PLAY** tab and select **Find a cache**. Enter your home address or starting point. You will see **Figure 16**. Then click on **MAP THE FIRST 1000 GEOCACHES** on the right side of the screen.

8. Zoom in and lick on the name of the cache if you are using step 6, or click on the cache icon if you are using step 7.

9. The cache page shows up; **Figure 17** is typical.

10. Look at the upper right side of the cache page for the words **LOG YOUR VISIT**. Click on that.

11. A new page appears, **Figure 18**.

12. Move your cursor over the **SELECT TYPE OF LOG** pull down menu and select **FOUND IT**, **DIDN'T FIND IT**, or **WRITE NOTE**.

   a) If you found the cache, select **FOUND IT**.

b) If you didn't find it but looked for a long time without success, then select **DIDN'T FIND IT**.

c) If you didn't find it but you didn't really try too hard either, or if you think the failure was due simply to lack of experience, you might want to consider simply writing a note. You might say something like: "Didn't find it, but I'm new to this. I will try again soon."

My Lists								
Geocache Name	Distance	Favorites	Size	Difficulty	Terrain	Last Found	Placed on
Century Marker TeamWalkers	0.5 mi W	5	Small	1.5	2.5	12/29/2016	01/14/2017
Scout Cache #7 Scout Troop 44	0.7 mi SE	4	Small	1.5	1.5	11/19/2016	04/01/2016
Blue Lizzie DogBoy	0.9 mi N	1	Micro	2.5	2.5	10/11/2016	09/10/2014
Lamp Post 3 Shelby Family	1.1 mi NW	11	Other	1.5	1.5	12/12/2016	12/30/2015
White Rock Rock Boy	1.2 mi N	2	Medium	3.5	3.0	07/21/2015	02/14/2011

Figure 16. List of caches from your starting point.

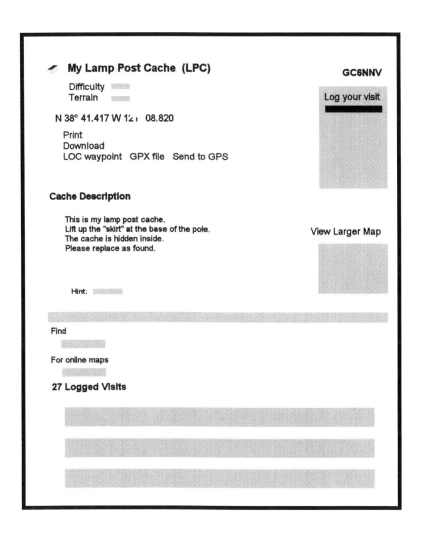

Figure 17. Typical cache page.

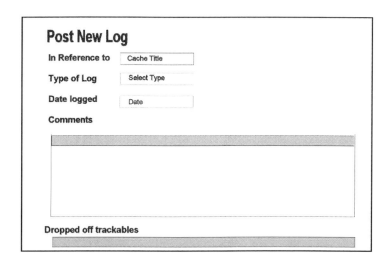

Figure 18. Post New Log window..

13. In either case, write a little something about what happened when you were looking for the cache. Cache owners love to see notes about what people think of their caches. If the container was entertaining or decorative then say so. If the hide location offered a beautiful view then write that too.

14. There are no set rules on what you have to say in a log entry, but you should at least make

note that you signed the log and you replaced the cache as you found it.

15. You should report if you left anything or took anything out of the cache.

16. If the log book or the container is damaged then say so in your comments.

17. Consider the etiquette and sportsmanship aspects of the log entry when you make comments. A brief entry might be simply "SL, TFTC" which means I signed the log. Thanks for the cache. How much more fun is it, however, if you give the log some pizzazz?!

    Consider writing something like this: "Wow! Had a great time hiking on the bike path and viewing all the great scenery around. Found the well-crafted cache after about 2 minutes and opened it up to see lots of goodies inside. I took a wooden nickel signature item and left a small figurine of a cat. The log book is clean and dry. Replaced as found. Very enjoyable adventure; Thank you!"

    That kind of log gives a shot in the arm to the cache owner and encourages other cachers to take the same hike along that bike path.

18. Check that the date on the log page is the actual date you made the find, or DNF.

19. If you found the cache and you picked up a trackable item, then you will have to log that too, as will be explained in a later chapter.

20. If you have your own trackable item and you dropped it off at the cache, there are boxes below the comments window where you can record dropping off your travel bug.

21. Click on **SUBMIT LOG ENTRY**.

22. Repeat the same steps for each cache that you found or did not find.

23. Congratulations; you are now an official geocacher!

NOTE: You can also log your cache finds from the map view by clicking on the caches you have found. See **Figure 19**.

Woo-Hoo! Give yourself a pat on the back!

Take a minute, too, to review what happened on your first trip. Do you want to bring bug spray next time, or a towel to wipe your hands? As your experience grows you will become more proficient at finding caches.

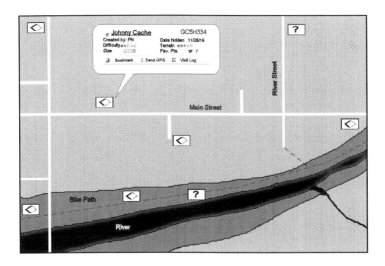

Figure 19. As an alternative, you can use the map-view page to click on and enter your cache log entries.

Chapter 9: Cache Types

Cache types

Up until this point our focus has been on traditional caches. There are many other cache types that provide really exciting and unusual adventures. Here we will examine some of the variations on the traditional cache type. See **Figure 20**.

Figure 20. Each cache type has its own icon. From left to right: Traditional cache, multi-cache, unknown cache, event cache, letterbox hybrid, Earthcache, virtual cache, CITO cache, mega event, and Wherigo.

Event caches

By far the most delightful cache type is the Event Cache. These are group gatherings where you can meet other geocachers in your area, find friends, exchange travel bugs, and have a good time. In addition, it all counts as a cache that you can log just as if you had found a cache container.

Event caches often include food, a group activity, or a public service, such as cleaning up a park. Event caches are HIGHLY RECOMMENDED activities, as it broadens your horizons and it's very entertaining. Event caches allow you to share experiences with like-minded adventurers.

A good example is the Flash Mob event, where people gather secretly at a public place, then on signal they do something silly, like sing a song, then disperse (after signing the event log).

There are different ways to find events in your area. When you sign up with Geocaching.com you automatically receive monthly bulletins which list upcoming events. Event caches also appear on the area maps as a little yellow dialog bubble.

Step-by-Step:
Selecting event caches

If you want to search for them on Geocaching.com, follow these steps.

1. Go online and navigate to Geocaching.com.

2. Click on the **COMMUNITY** tab and select **Events**.

3. Scroll down towards the bottom of the page and you will see a **CALENDAR OF EVENTS**.

4. For the day you are interested in, click on the date number at the top of the column.

5. International events are listed first. Scroll down to your state and click on the events in your area to read about them.

Be prepared to have some fun! Each cache type has its own symbol which appears on the map view. Again, see **Figure 20**.

Traditional caches

Traditional caches have been discussed already.

Geocaching.com defines it as follows: "This is the original geocache type consisting of, at minimum, a container and a log book or logsheet. Larger containers generally include items for trade. **Nano** or **Micro** caches are tiny containers that only hold a logsheet. The coordinates listed on the traditional cache page provide the geocache's exact location." The small nano caches often have a built-in magnet to help them stick to metal pieces.

Multi-cache

A multi-cache has different parts or stages. At the first stage you find instructions or clues to the next stage. This repeats until you come to the last stage where the actual cache and log are located. Some multi-caches have only two steps. Some of them have coordinates for the next phase while others list instructions, such as "Follow the brick path until you see a large tree stump."

Virtual cache

A virtual cache does not have a physical container or a log to sign. Instead, you travel to the location and make the observations required by the cache web page. A virtual cache might be a physical structure, such as a roller coaster, or a statue of a great person, and you are required to record specific information to prove that you visited the site. As an example, the statue might have a commemorative plaque attached which tells you who the sculptor was, what date the statue was put in place, and who helped place it there.

Virtual caches are being phased out, so no new ones of this type will appear in the future.

Letterbox hybrid cache

Letterboxing is a sport which is very similar to geocaching, although you don't need a GPS unit for letterboxing. The Letterbox is a hidden box that you find, like a treasure hunt, by following a set of instructions. This hobby is so similar to geocaching that the Letterboxes that are registered as caches are called Letterbox Hybrid Caches. They are often geared towards younger players, although adults generally enjoy the activity just as much. Letterbox caches usually have more than one stage to complete before you find the final treasure.

The web presence for letterboxing is located at http://www.letterboxing.org/. The hobby of letterboxing generally includes making or buying a personal rubber stamp and ink pad. When you find the letterbox you are supposed to impress your stamp onto the log book inside the letterbox. You also can record the rubber stamp that is inside the letterbox to your own log book of stamp impressions that you carry with you. This way both you and the letterbox owner have a large collection of stamp impressions.

Unknown (puzzle) cache

Unknown caches generally involve a puzzle or riddle that you have to solve to find the cache. This category of caches includes a wide variety of head-scratching games, quizzes, and tricks that you have to figure out to find the cache location. This is, if you'll pardon the pun, a catch-all category for geocaches.

Puzzle caches are really fun and will keep your mind active. Most are pretty easy to solve but some can be quite difficult.

Example 1: You are sent to a starting point where you have to look around and find the street address of the nearest building. You are instructed to add the street number to the West coordinates of the starting point, and then subtract the same number from the North coordinates. The new coordinates point to where the cache is located.

Example 2. The puzzle cache name is Goblet of Fire, one of the Harry Potter books. You are asked "What age was Harry when he learned he was a wizard?" and "What is the 'Age of Majority' in the wizarding world?" These answers can be found by reading the book or checking the Goblet of Fire Wikipedia site on the internet. (The answers are 11 and 17 respectively.) You are then instructed to walk exactly 11 feet in one direction and 17 feet in another direction to find the actual cache site.

Earth cache

An Earth Cache is very similar to a virtual cache in that there is no container or log to sign. Similarly, you have to record specific information to prove you visited the site. As the name implies Earth Cache sites have geological or environmental significance which is quite often tremendously interesting. An Earth Cache might be at a fish hatchery or a meteor impact site. The information is generally available from signs, posters, or information booths at the site.

Miscellaneous cache types

There are several other cache types that are not as popular as the ones listed above. Meanwhile, Geocaching.com will sometimes add or delete a cache category. The ones that are rarely used or hard to find are:

Project APE caches: Caches with Planet of the Apes theme.

Webcam caches: A cache where you appear on a public web camera and someone records your visit. Webcam caches are being phased out, so no new ones of this type will appear in the future.

GPS adventures exhibit: GPS Adventures Mazes are designed to teach people of all ages about GPS technology and geocaching through interactive science experiences.

Wherigo caches: Wherigo is a stand-alone device using game cartridges for creating and playing GPS-enabled adventures in the real world.

For the latest information on cache types see: http://www.geocaching.com/about/cache_types.aspx.

Below is a list of the various cache type. To select any of these, do the following.

Step-by-Step:
Selecting specific cache types

1. Connect your GPS to your computer using the USB cable. The computer should recognize your GPS device as described above.

2. Sign on to Geocaching.com. Click on the Play tab at the top and select Find a Cache.

3. Enter your street address or the address where you want to start looking for caches.

4. Click on the Add Filter box. You will see **Figure 21.**

5. Use the slider on the upper right to select the Difficulty and Terrain you want to experience.

6. Check boxes next to the cache types you want to explore.

7. Click on the Search box.

8. You will see a list of caches in your area of the type caches you selected.

9. Examine each one and see if you want to add them to your next adventure.

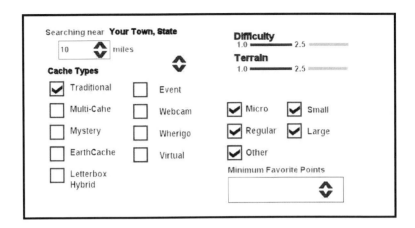

Figure 21. Selecting caches with filters showing check marks for Traditional and Event caches.

Chapter 10:
The Journeyman

Advancing from beginner to experienced geocacher

This book is designed to get you started in geocaching. If you've completed the previous chapters you are probably getting to know how to play the game. The biggest booster to the hobby is to join other geocachers, and attend geocaching events to improve your caching skills.

The best teacher is experience. As the number count of your found caches increases you will come across more complex caches, unusual hiding places, and creative cache containers. If you have any trouble, don't be shy to contact other geocachers who have found the cache that you may be having trouble with.

Geocaching is a wide open sport and things are changing every day. A good source for answering technical questions is the Geocaching Learn page, the first tab on the main page. See: http://www.geocaching.com/guide/.

Another good source, and a place to ask questions, is the Geocaching.com discussion forum which is handled by Groundspeak. See: http://forums.groundspeak.com/GC//.

Videos can also teach you a lot about geocaching. There are videos on geocaching at http://www.geocaching.com/videos/. You may also find a wide range of tutorials and adventures on popular video websites such as YouTube.com.

Circulating your own travel bugs

After geocaching for a while maybe you've been lucky enough to find a travel bug in one of the caches. These are little figurines, toys, or gadgets that have a travel bug coin, tag, or marker with a serial number used to track the object. The idea is to keep the item moving from cache to cache. If you own one you can look up a map of all the places the bug has traveled to. Actually, you can view the map of any travel bug for which you have the tracking number.

To view the page for any travel bug, simply enter Geocaching.com, select Play, and click on the FIND TRAVEL BUGS listing in the pull-down menu. Enter the tracking number in the box labeled ENTER THE TRACKING CODE OF THE ITEM and press return.

About the center of the page you'll see the VIEW MAP link. When you click on that you will see a map of all the caches this particular travel bug has visited.

Now imagine if this were your own travel bug! You might drop it off while on vacation in another state, and you can see where it goes and who retrieved it.

To get started with trackable items you first have to buy a travel bug. They are sometimes referred to as travel tags, geocoins, or simply trackables: see **Figure 22**. Different companies produce and sell them. You can find travel bug sales on Geocaching.com by selecting the SHOPPING tab.

You will see a new page with TRACKABLES as one of the new tabs, near the center of the top of the page.

Figure 22. Travel Bugs and trackable items come in all shapes and sizes. The top two are trackable travel bugs. At bottom left is a "wooden nickel souvenir. Bottom right is geo-coin.

You can also find trackable items for sale at other websites. For example:

- http://www.coinsandpins.com/

- http://www.cacheboxstore.com/

- http://www.gpscity.com/

- http://www.thecachestation.com/categories/ Travel-Tags/

- http://www.mygeogear.com/

Once you've purchased a trackable item you have to register it with Geocaching.com in order to create a tracking page. Some trackable items provide the activation code packaged with the item. For other distributors, such as CoinsAndPins.com you can retrieve the tracking code at the seller's web site. This is called activating the trackable. It then links you to the Geocaching.com site so you can register it there.

To register a travel bug, navigate to Geocaching.com; click on **PLAY** and select **FIND TRACKABLES**, then enter the tracking code and the activation code in the appropriate boxes.

Once you've registered the trackables you have to fill out a Geocaching.com form which tells everyone what the mission of the trackable is. You may want to upload a photo of the item too.

When the paperwork is done you can drop the trackable item off at any cache that is large enough to hold it. After registering, the trackable is automatically added to your personal inventory on Geocaching.com. Then, when you log your cache visit, you will see a box near the bottom of the cache page where you can check **DROPPED OFF**. The cache page will then show your trackable in its cache inventory on the right side of the page.

After that you simply check your trackables page to see when and where it has traveled. Every time someone moves your item you will receive an email notification. Have fun!

Hiding your own caches

Hiding your own cache is actually an advanced subject, but once you get into the swing of geocaching, sooner or later you will want to hide your own cache.

Be advised, you should have found at least 100 caches from other people before you start thinking of hiding your own. Since this is complex process and not for beginners we will list only a broad outline of the steps.

1. Create your cache container. Start simple. Bison tubes, which you can buy at many of the suppliers listed in the Appendix make great containers. Consider using a plastic film canister or washed out mayonnaise jar.

2. Take photographs of your container and the place where you expect to hide it. In order to post a picture to the Geocaching.com site you must have a direct link to the photo. Some, but not all photo hosting websites will provide the direct link for you. Photobucket.com and Tinypic.com are popular examples.

3. It's best to prepare your cache description before you go on line. Write up the details using a word processor on your computer so you can simply cut and paste the words into the forms displayed.

4. On Geocaching.com click on **PLAY** and select **HIDE AND SEEK A CACHE**. The **HIDE A CACHE** box on the right includes several links to help you get started. Be sure to read and understand the **CACHE LISTING REQUIREMENTS AND GUIDELINES** link. The hardest part is finding an area to hide your cache that is 1/10-th mile or more from any

surrounding caches. The geocaching.com page will guide you through this part with a map showing your chosen location versus nearby caches. Nearby caches are shown as green circles. Your new cache must fall outside the pre-existing green circles.

5. Once you are ready with your cache, your description, the location coordinates, and your photos, you can fill out the **ONLINE FORM** by clicking on that link. You may fill out most of it and come back later to complete the process.

6. Once the form is filled out, click on the Preview button to be sure everything looks the way you want it to. The next step is to submit it for review and you will be notified when it is posted.

Hiding caches comes with a responsibility to maintain the cache properly, as explained by the descriptions in geocaching.com. Good luck!

Exploring beyond Geocaching.com

Although Geocaching.com is by far the most popular website for geocaching enthusiasts, there are many other sites that center around geocaching and GPS related activities. Some of these are listed below.

1. **Waymarking** is similar to virtual caches on Geocaching.com. Waymarks are sights and locations that you find with a GPS device and log your visits online. Generally you must take a photograph to prove you visited the site. See http://www.waymarking.com/default.aspx?f=1.

2. **Navicache** is a site similar to Geocaching.com. They have different icons and require a separate sign-in. See http://www.navicache.com/.

3. **Terracaching** is also similar to Geocaching.com. The Terracaching site lists caches that are not necessarily listed with other sites. For example Geocaching caches are required to be a tenth of a mile distant from each other, but there may be a Terracache closer. See http://www.Terracaching.com.

4. **Open Caching.** Opencaching, like Terracaching is independent of Geocaching.com, so some caches may be listed here that are not on other sites, and they too may be closer than 1/10th mile from caches on Geocaching.com.
See: http://www.opencaching.us/index.php.

2. **GPSgames** offers several activities that rely on your GPS unit. There are games such as Geodashing, Geogolf, and Shutterspot. An example from their website:
"Shutterspot is a game in which some players take photographs and other players are challenged to find the exact spot where the photographer stood when the camera shutter clicked. That's the 'Shutterspot'."
See: http://www.gpsgames.org.

3. **Earthcache** is a site dedicated to Earthcaches and is a partner with Geocaching.com. See: http://www.earthcache.org/.

4. **Handicaching** is a site for the handicapped or those who want low difficulty caches. Caches are ranked by users for terrain and accessibility.
See: http://www.handicaching.com/.

11. Geocaching Resources

Geocaching websites

THE major site for geocaching is Geocaching.com, the largest and most respected resource for this hobby. They also have an excellent discussion forum at forums.groundspeak.com/GC/.

Groundspeak is the umbrella organization for Geocaching.com, Waymarking.com (virtual caches), Wherigo.com, and CITO, the Cache-In, Trash Out adjunct to geocaching.

These interconnected website URLs are as follows

- http://www.geocaching.com/

- http://www.groundspeak.com/

- http://www.waymarking.com/

Geocaching-related websites

Garmin: http://www8.garmin.com/outdoor/geocaching/

Buxleys Geocaching Waypoint:
http://brillig.com/geocaching/

Open Caching: http://www.opencaching.com/en/

TerraCaching: http://www.terracaching.com/

Letterboxing: http://www.letterboxing.org

http://www.handicaching.com/

http://www.navicache.com/

http://www.waymarking.com/default.aspx?f=1

http://www.GPSGames.org

http://www.Earthcache.org

Magazines

- FTF Geocacher: http://www.ftfgeocacher.com/
- Online Geocacher: http://onlinegeocacher.com/

Major manufacturers

- DeLorme: http://www.delorme.com/

- Garmin: http://www.garmin.com/us/

- Lowrance:
  http://www.lowrance.com/Products/Outdoor/

- Magellan: http://www.magellangps.com/

Discussion forums

- Groundspeak:
  http://gpsunderground.com/forum/forum.php

- GPS Passion:
  http://www.gpspassion.com/forumsen/

- GPS Review: http://forums.gpsreview.net/

- http://project-gc.com/forum/list?8

Geocaching supplies

- http://www.coinsandpins.com/

- http://www.cacheboxstore.com/

- http://www.gpscity.com/

- http://stores.geowyrm.com/

- http://www.crazycaches.com/

- http://shop4swag.com/catalog/

- http://www.cache-advance.com/

- http://spacecoastgeocachers.com/

- http://ibgeocaching.com/

Appendix A
– Simple Cache Containers

This section is designed to present projects and ideas for making functional containers and hides for geocaching. If you love geocaching as much as I do, then sooner or later you will want to make a contribution to the hobby by creating an enjoyable experience for others.

John Lennon, the philosophical songwriter for The Beatles, once wrote "In the end, the love you take is equal to the love you make." The same is true for our hobby: you get out of it just about what you put into it. In geocaching, one of the most enjoyable adventures is to find a cache that brings a smile to the searcher's face, or perhaps a raised eyebrow for the craftsmanship that went into its construction. If you want to just get by with minimal effort, then wash out an old mayonnaise jar, but if you want to elevate the sport and spread the cheer of creating a memorable cache, then take the little effort required to make a truly creative cache container.

Fun for the searcher

Many factors contribute to making a memorable cache. It might be that the name of the street and the type of container match each other, such as an apple-shaped jar hidden on McIntosh Street. It might be that the route to the location takes you past an awesome vista. Or it might be that the mental gymnastics needed to solve a field puzzle gives an extra punch to the cache. All such considerations help make the experience enjoyable, but one of the biggest fun factors is making an eye-caching or clever container.

Containers can be fun, frivolous, crafty, or mechanical. They should enhance the geocaching experience by adding variety and artistry to the hiding place. Even a simple upgrade makes a big difference, **Figure A-1**.

Design Considerations

Many practical matters can limit our creativity, such as the expense, the availability of materials, time considerations, and the crafting skills of the cache owner.

In addition to creative ideals, we have to think about the following design concerns:

- Waterproofing. Water contamination is probably the most common problem facing cache owners. Even with sealable containers, water often works its way in and makes for a soggy log. Waterproof papers are now available, but they are expensive. A good solution to the water problem is to add layers of protection. You might, for example, have a bird house as the outer layer and camouflage exterior, then have a Tupperware container inside the bird house, and then again have the log sealed inside a plastic bag.

- Stealth. You want your cache to be searchable and recognizable by the geocacher, but mundane enough to pass as an ordinary part of the environment for non-cachers (muggles).

- Accessibility. The cache may endure quite a bit of traffic, so the container must open and close easily, have a decent seal, and be hidden in such a way it can easily be returned to its hiding place.

- Sturdiness. The cache must hold contents securely, be able to withstand weather and mechanical buffeting, and survive long enough to minimize changing of the container.

- Ease of Production. Creativity is great, but not always practical. I found a hollow log in a pet store that costs only $12.00. It was made for the bubble-maker for fish tanks. It might take 3 or 4 hours to hollow out the same sized log with drills and chisels, but the store bought version works just as well in hiding the container.

With these considerations in mind, the next step is to honestly assess your level of skill and patience with mechanical processes, such as drilling holes, soldering, or painting. Although it's good once in a while to stretch yourself, it's also wise to know your limits. If you don't know how to change the blades on a Dremmel tool (or even know what a Dremmel tool is), then you might want to stick with buying a simple Tupperware container and using your artistic skills to paint a design on the outside. On the other hand, if you have a 3-car garage converted to a world class wood shop, then you can go ahead and tackle something more creative.

Figure A-1. Containers don't have to be complicated to be interesting. Here a jar inside a tin or a vegetable holder with eyes glued onto it does the trick.

1. The Bison Tube

A bison tube is a small metal cylinder with a screw-off top and waterproof seal. It can range in size from about 3/8-inch wide and 2-3/8-inch long to 1-inch wide and 3-inches long. The most common size is a half inch wide and 2-3/4-inch long. Thus, it can usually hold nothing but a rolled up log sheet. The tubes come with a key chain type slip ring, so they are easily attached to other objects.

Bison tubes generally cost about a dollar each, with large discounts for bulk purchases. They have a very small rubber seal that can wear out in a short time. This can compromise its waterproofing ability. These tubes are best used where a second layer of protection can be added against the rain. For example, you can put them inside a steel fence post cap or inside a piece of PVC pipe.

Figure A-2 shows some ways to make the hide more interesting. At top, a metal fence post cap has been drilled to take a #6 machine screw and nut, which is glued on the inside and attached by a plastic tie. You don't really need to drill a hole it the top, as the glue generally holds well, but a mechanical connection is always better than glue alone.

In the center is a hack-sawed railroad tie with a bison tube attached to the end. Old, rusty railroad ties can be found on line, or if you're lucky and live in a town with an abandoned rail line you can find them at nearby flea markets. Obviously, do not hide or retrieve anything on an active rail line.

To make a railroad spike cache, prop the railroad tie into a vise and cut it in half with a hacksaw. Next saw a groove in the cut end. Insert a wire in the groove then put masking tape around the end. This holds the wire in place and forms a cup for the glue. Pour in epoxy or gorilla glue to provide an anchor for the wire that holds the bison tube.

At the bottom, a bison tube is placed inside a toy rubber duck. It doesn't take much effort to find toys and fun items to act as outer camouflage for the bison tubes.

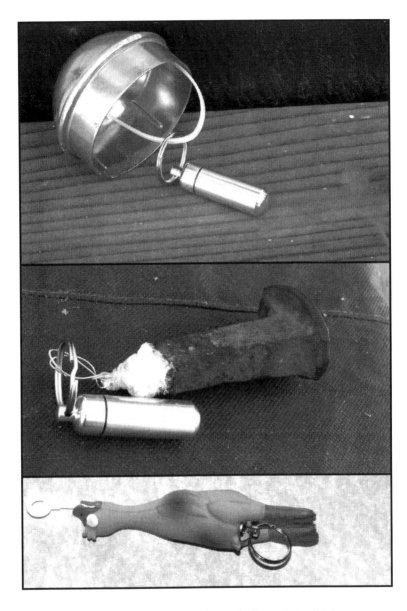

Figure A-2. These are examples of bison tube hides.

Bison tubes are pretty versatile, as they fit inside many outdoor objects, such as pipes, fences, knotholes in trees, and as a hanger on bushes. A bison tube is easily made into a hanger by wrapping a bread tie or a paper clip through the slip ring and hanging it on the inner limb of a tree or shrubbery.

A variation on the bison tube is the "nano" tube. These are generally much smaller, about a half-inch long and a quarter-inch wide. They contain tiny rolled up log sheets which often require a tweezers to remove from the cylinder. They are usually magnetic and will stick to the back of a traffic sign, under a bench, or attached to any metallic surface.

Nano tubes get mixed reviews from geocachers. On the one hand, being so small they are easy to hide in urban settings and can be a challenge to find. On the other hand, they don't allow trading of travel bugs and the logs fill up quickly.

2. Film Canister

A film canister refers to the plastic 35-mm film containers most photographers are familiar with. The black film containers are constructed of high density polyethylene (HDPE) plastic, a tough, commonly used semi-rigid material. Its flexibility allows the cap to be pushed on and removed by hand for a decent seal against moisture. Like the bison tubes, it's best to provide an extra layer of protection against moisture. This category includes other common containers of similar size. **Figure A-3** shows a slightly smaller medical supply container with a flip-top cap. This is recycled from the can for diabetic test strips.

Containers for 35-mm film are 1-7/8-inch long and 7/8 inch in diameter. These containers are quite common in geocahing. You can simply add a bent paper clip and some camouflage tape and have an instant hanging hide. Hopefully we can take it one step further and make something interesting out of it.

One of the easiest things you can do is paint a face on the cap, or the entire body, to make it look like a bug or animal. If the lid is the face of a cat, for example, you can glue on eyes and whiskers. I find epoxy glue works best for this type of add-on.

You can also insert the film canister into a toy, into a camouflaging object, or simply attach it to the back of a model truck as in the photo.

Figure A-3. There are several methods of spicing up a simple film canister cache.

112

3. Food Jar

Jars are probably the most popular form of container for geocaching. Cleaned up mayonnaise and peanut butter jars are most common, as they come in large sizes and have a lid, or mouth, that is as wide as the jar itself. They provide good water-proofing and the only cost you endure is washing out the last vestiges of food content.

A crucial variable with jars is that they must have a good seal to keep out water. Many good jars have spongy plastic or rubber cushioning that seals against water as you tighten the lid. Some plastic jars can be quite thin and corrode over time. It's best to pick a jar with a good seal and think walls.

Plastic versus glass jars

I know glass is frowned upon because of the danger of breakage, but some jars are quite thick and strong, and many environments, such as deserts and deep forest have few rock hazards that pose a danger of breakage. The rule of thumb is to use plastic instead of glass. Just imagine your search area covered with chards of broken glass and you get the idea.

Glass can be stronger and more durable and you might choose that route IF:

- The glass is tempered and tough, like Pyrex®.

- The entire container is covered with a layer or two of protective tape.

- The glass container is completely surrounded by a protective outer layer, such as a glass jar inside a wooden birdhouse.

In a nutshell, the glass jar must be protected in such a way that even if it breaks the chards will not pose a danger. You can assist in this goal by embedding it in an outer protective shell, such as a wooden frame.

Pyrex is a registered trademark of Corning, Inc., Corning, NY.

Figure A-4. Plastic containers and jars come in all sizes.

115

Figure A-4 shows some examples of jars. At top is a pop-up lid container, a metal screw cap on a glass jar, and medicine bottle-sized plastic screw top container.

The middle illustration shows the inner lining which provides the seal against water. The bottom illustrates the difficulty with jars – that is, they are hard to dress up and make interesting. Sometimes the best you can do is simply to cover them with a toy or outer mask. The bottom portion of the photo shows jars covered with patterned duct tape.

Here are some ideas for making the containers more interesting:

- Paint a scene on the inside of the plastic container, then seal the design with urethane spray to protect it.

- Cover the jar with duct tape or camouflage tape. Duct tape now comes in several different colors and designer patterns, such as leopards' skin and zebra stripes.

- Use craft wire to add legs, arms, antennas and such to the outside, and secure it with a good quality glue, such as epoxy.

Have fun. Jars represent a quick and easy way to get started with your first cache hide.

4. Food Storage Container

Food storage containers are popular cache holders. We are referring to plastic sealable containers such as Tupperware® and Rubbermaid®. One of the most popular types of food containers for caches is known as Lock & Lock which has sealing latches on all four sides of the lid. The chief advantages of this type of cache are their excellent seal against moisture, and the variety of sizes they come in. Another advantage is that they are easily covered with paint or camouflage material.

Rubbermaid is a registered trademark of Rubbermaid Commercial Products, Inc, Wooster, OH. **Tupperware is a registered trademark** of DART Industries, Inc., Orlando, FL.

Variations

The four-edged Lock & Lock type containers are produced by other manufacturers as shown in **Figure A-5**. In the center photo, a Pyrex® cup is shown with a sealable rubber lid. The bottom portion shows 4-latch sealed containers in the field, the left one painted a camouflage color and the right left unaltered.

Figure A-5. Food storage containers make good caches.

5. Military Ammunition Can

The ammo can, or ammunition container, is a classic and popular cache hide. It has a relatively large storage capacity and it's rugged and waterproof.

There are several variations on the ammo can. Some are original World War II surplus containers. These generally have poor water seals that have dried out over the years. Fortunately they are easy to repair with thin weather stripping. Although they provide a fairly good seal, water often does find a way to get into the box. Some are modern plastic versions which are not as strong as the metal type. Others are odd sizes for different calibers of ammunition.

The standard size is the classic .50 caliber M2A1 which is 7 1/4" high, 5 3/4" wide, and 11" long, **Figure A-6**. They weigh about 5 pound each or a little more for shipping purposes. The other standard sizes you might see are .30 caliber, 25mm, 40mm, or the "tall" version which is 6" by 11" by 13".

Hiding the Ammo Can

The ammo can, being fairly large, is a favorite for geocachers who want to trade items or to make a cache that will serve as a travel-bug hotel. The upside of large containers is that they can hold much more interesting trade and swag items, but the downside is that they are more easily discovered by passers-by, or "muggles" who might compromise the hide.

Swag is a short-hand word for the toys and tradable items found it caches. It comes from S.W.A.G, meaning stuff we all get, referring to the gifts that celebrities receive at red-carpet events. **Muggles**, the term used in Harry Potter movies for non-wizards, refers to people who are not aware that the enclosure is part of the geocaching game.

Since the ammo box is so large, it's important to hide it among rocks or vegetation that can help conceal its square outline. A good way to both hide it and make it simple is to use a mask type cover, such as the wraps described elsewhere, **Chapter 18**. In **Figure 6** I used sheet metal flowers to hide the cache. You'd be surprised how effective something that simple is when used in the field.

A more thorough way to hide the box is to surround it with rocks or cover the top with moss or other artificial flower type decorations.

Figure A-6. Top: Ammo boxes have a lever-like latch.
Bottom: Simple metal foil wrap works well in the woods.

6. Water Bottles and Thermos Containers

Sports-type water bottles, seal-top coffee mugs and thermos containers are everywhere. They make great cache hide because they seal well, are relatively rugged, and are inexpensive.

Sports drink containers, water bottles, thermos cups and the like are everywhere and are easily converted to a waterproof cache. The only difficulty is that most of them have a flip up spout or opening for a straw that has to be sealed up. That leaves just the screw-off top to provide access to the cache. For me the glue of choice is epoxy.

Many of these containers have hooks (for a bicycle) or clips that can be used as hangers for the cache. They come in a variety of colors, so black or green will help with concealment. As with jars and other off-the-shelf containers the trick here is to add something to the outside to make it more appealing, more camouflaged, or more theme-specific for the searcher.

Simple Camouflage

Figure A-7 shows two unadorned drink containers at the top; the left one made of metal and the right a simple flip-top plastic container. You will notice the plastic container also has a screw-off lid. Both have hooks convenient for hanging.

At the bottom left is a small thermos completely covered in camouflage tape, and at the bottom right a two-layer coffee mug with a ghost figurine attached to the top. The same glue that secures the figurine to the top also seals the flip-up spout shut.

Figure A-7. Sport drink containers and thermos bottles make great caches.

There are two basic approaches to make the plain containers more interesting. First, you can add colored tape to the outside, paint the outside with designs, such as teeth or a face, or add texture with thick paint and additions, such as glitter or sand. The second approach is to add objects to the outside that transform the shape or appearance. For example you can add wire legs to make it look like a bug, or wings to make it look like a bird or plane. If the container is going to hang in a bush or a tree, simply adding artificial leaves or bark to the outside will completely transform its appearance.

The trouble with adding things like legs to the outside is the difficulty of attaching objects to hard, durable surfaces such as metal or plastic. I find it best to add secure anchors, such as copper wire or plastic zip ties to the outside then apply a waterproof glue to keep them in place. You can then attach decorations to the wire or zip ties.

7. Toy Cache Containers

Toys make great cache containers because the shape and purpose of the toy easily lends itself to an amusing hiding place. You can use a child's action figure to hold a container and that's enough to make it interesting. You can use the space inside toys to hide more traditional containers.

A Quick and Simple Transformation

Sturdy plastic or rubber toys are good for hides. I particularly like dog toys and pool toys because they are generally rugged and nearly waterproof.

The very simplest arrangement is to attach a toy to a container, making it appear the toy is carrying or riding the container. In the photo below **Figure A-8**, a toy cricket is holding a screw-top jar, and a tree face toy mold shows you can transform any container into a cartoon-like head. These tree faces are found in garden stores. Similar faces are made for pumpkins at Halloween.

In the lower part of the photograph a rubber dog toy in the shape of a tree is easily modified to hold a plastic jar. The bottom portion of the dog's throw toy is cut open to remove the squeaker, and a hole is punched in the top to add a hanger wire. The toy is in the shape of a tree limb, so this would work well for hides within the branches of a tree.

This type of cache is super-simple and quick to make. The rubber is stiff and durable enough that even with the split in the bottom the toy retains its shape and closes over onto the container.

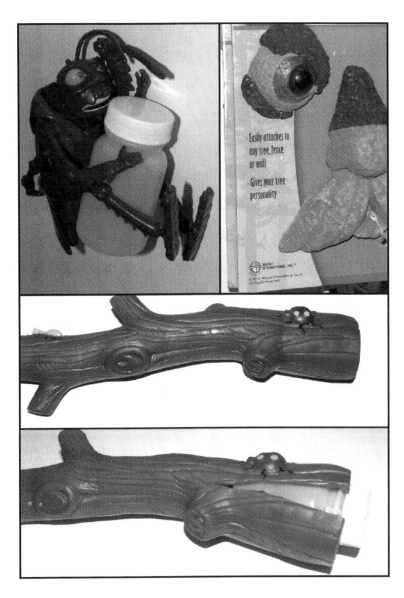

Figure A-8. You can make quick and easy conversions of toys for cache hides.

8. PVC Tubing Cache

If you haven't worked with PVC tubing before, you're in for a treat. PVC, short for polyvinyl chloride, is a light-weight material that lends itself well to cache hides because it is cheap, easy to cut, and it comes in a variety of sizes. In addition, the ends of the tube can be covered with a slip-on cap or a threaded lid that provides a water tight seal.

Most people are familiar with the ½-inch and ¾-inch tubing used for home sprinkler systems. These of course are adequate for hiding small bison tubes or nano containers. There are, however, much larger sizes, such as 3-inch to over 12-inch diameter pipes. When you combine that with the pre-fitted end caps and the ability to cut the pipe to any length, you can see this is a good solution for custom cache sizes.

You can also easily paint PVC, drill holes for handles and attachments, and use adapters to transition from one size to another. Another advantage is that PVC piping is so common that when you position it next to a utility box or construction site, it seems to fit right in, looking like a part of the facility engineering.

The basic container

I find that the standard black 3-inch black (sewer pipe) is a great way to start. The black color blends in easily, and the 3-inch size is still pretty inexpensive. Spend some time in the hardware store looking at all the attachments and gismos that go with the basic design. The minimum you'll need is a section of tubing, a slip-on cap for one end, and a screw-on cap for the other end. You will need to buy a small tube of PVC glue, as well, to seal the slip-on cap in place. Since the basic pipe does not come with a threaded end, you will have to buy a slip-on cap with a threaded interior, and a threaded plug to allow geocachers to open the container. You can use an unglued slip on cap for the open end too, but it will not be as watertight as the screw cap.

If you want to seal one end permanently, use a small can of PVC glue. Select a medium grade, such as the green can.

Figure A-9. PVC piping and connectors come in various sizes.

131

Figure A-9 shows some of the many shapes for the ¾-inch PVC pipes, with an elbow, an end cap, and an extension connector that has one slip-on side and one side that's threaded to take a threaded plug. The great advantage of PVC caches is that you can choose large size tubes, as show in the lower portion of the photograph. Here the familiar sewer pipe access cap is pictured, the classic black version as well as a white alternative. You might want to consider buying a flange connector too for the bottom of the tube. It allows you to mount the pipe on any piece of wood, so that when you deposit the cache in the wild, it looks as if it's a utility pipe coming out of the ground.

9. False Sprinkler

False sprinkler heads are a fairly common hiding place for caches, but they remain quite popular. Essentially, you take out the insides of the sprinkler head, seal the top and bottom ends, and you have a simple screw-off top container for hiding items. The sprinklers come in all different sizes, so you can choose a larger one if you want to fit more inside.

There are some warnings you should remember if you choose this method. First, don't damage private property or public lands. This means you will have to either be the owner or get written permission from the owner to dig the hole where the sprinkler will be placed. Second, the sprinkler head has two openings, one at the top and one at the bottom, and both need to be sealed. Finally, if there is a garden or shrubbery around, you want to warn seekers not to trample plants or vegetation in their search.

If you're not familiar with sprinklers, get an old or broken one to play with. They are designed to let water in from the bottom, connected to underground PVC piping, and spray it out the top. Sprinkler heads come in all different lengths and diameters. Remember, you will have to dig a hole to place the device, so consider that when choosing a size.

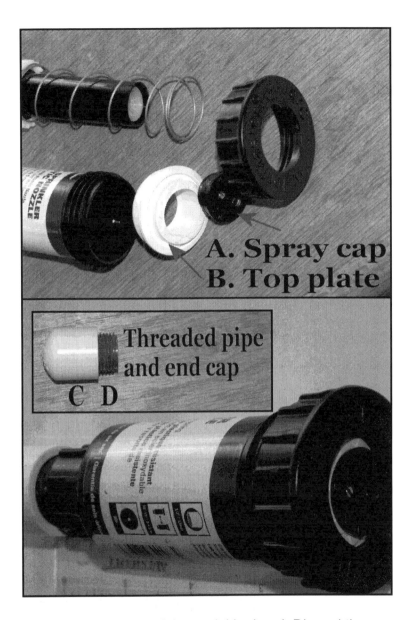

A. Spray cap
B. Top plate

Threaded pipe and end cap
C   D

Figure A-10. This is a false sprinkler head. Discard the riser and the spring, but save the cap and the cover pieces (top). Seal the bottom end with threaded tubing and cap.

There is a spring-loaded riser inside, and as you unscrew the top, the spring will push the riser channel out. And yes, you can knock your eye out.

Unscrew the top and remove the riser and spring. The riser tube has a simple screw-off spray cap. Remove that from the riser tube. Discard the riser tube and the spring that surrounds it. There may also be a top plate in the removable cap. See **Figure A-10,** items A and B. Replace the cap into the top plate and pour a small amount of epoxy glue into it to seal the holes. Set that aside and let the glue dry.

You will have to buy a small section of threaded PVC tubing and a threaded cap for the bottom end to seal it. See **Figure 10**, items C and D. Hand tighten the bottom to seal that end. When the glue is dry on the top part, simply screw on the lid again and you're good to go. You will have to dig a small hole in the ground to place it. You want just the top of the sprinkler to be visible.

Now, if you're incredibly lazy – and I shouldn't even mention this – there are ready-make key hiders in the shape of a phony sprinkler head available in many hardware stores. These are truly ready to go and the ends are sealed already, but they don't look as authentic as the re-engineered ones we've just described.

10. Key Holder

Key holders or hiders refer to those containers you can buy at most hardware stores that are designed to hide a spare set of keys for your house. They are usually in the shape of a rock, yard animal, or a simple metal box that has magnets on the back. This category includes other common off-the-shelf products, such as hollow rocks, light weight boulders for hiding a garden hose, or flower pots in the shape of stones and animals.

This type of cache is the lazy man's solution to hiding a cache, and you generally don't have to do much to improve its appearance. The key-hide containers are usually not waterproof, so you will need to add another inside container or at least a sealable plastic bag for the log book.

There are some easy fixes for the magnetic key holder. One simple improvement is to blot out the manufacturer's logo with black paint and add white stick-on numbers to the front. Cover this with a couple layers of spray-on urethane for moisture protection. The letters allow you to stick the box right onto any metallic surface and it looks like a registration or identification number.
See **Figure A-11** top.

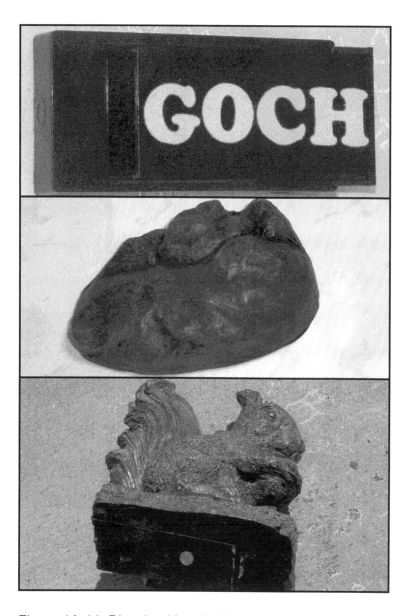

Figure 1A-11. Disguised key holders come in many shapes, including the standard magnetic key holder, dog-doo hide, and garden animal.

137

The hollow rock and dog-doo key holders probably don't need any adjustments. If they are hidden among rocks or debris of the same color they will blend in nicely. See **Figure A-11** center. If you want to add a personal touch, look for "textured" spray paints. These are extra thick spray cans, about $6.00 each, that leave a textured finish. The same holds true for the larger false boulders designed to cover hoses or utility meters. These are generally recognized as props once you are close up, but in a field of similar rock or landscape materials, they can be great places to hide caches.

There are also quite a number of garden animal key holders, such as turtles, squirrels, and gnomes that double as key holders. See **Figure A-11** bottom. Again, these don't need much work, but they are generally small and can hold only a log and the smallest swag items, such as coins.

11. Hollowed Out Log

The idea here is to hide a cache in the woods using a wooden log that mimics a broken or cut limb of a tree. The cache then is placed with other logs, branches and debris so that it blends in with the environment.

This can be a difficult project because wood is tough, heavy, and it can splinter and crack.

There are many different ways to accomplish the tree limb hide, and before we start it's helpful to consider some of the variables involved. If you can find a log that is hollow inside and not too rotted out, that would save a lot of time. If you have a half dozen power tools and a work bench out in the garage, then that too will make quick work of the woodworking part.

General strategy

The general plan is to insert a waterproof container inside of a tree limb so that its visibility is obscured and the log plays a camouflage role for the cache, **Figure A-12**. As mentioned, if you can find a small hollow log, then half your work is done already. All you would need to do is clear out and clean the core of the log and find a container that will fit.

If you have to start with a limb cut from a tree, the approach is to use a chain saw to cut a section out of the main branch, sawing it length-wise, and then hollow out a section to hold an internal container. You would attach that section back on with metal hinges, so it closes over the container. You can use a hand saw instead of a chain saw, but it will take much more time and effort.

Specific plan

This particular project starts with a downed tree, and one limb is saved before it goes into the recycling bin. Don't try to tackle any limb more than 4 or 5 inches thick, unless you happen to have a lumberjack in the family.

Saw the stump lengthwise down the middle. Mark out a square on each half that is slightly larger than the container you plan to hide inside. You can mark with a felt pen, or if you have a rotary tool, such as a Dremmel saw, you can pre-cut an outline down to about ¼ inch. You need to leave at least ½ inch from each edge for structural purposes.

If you have a router you can make quick work of digging out a center hole. If you don't know what a router is, then continue with the chisel method.

Figure A-12. A waterproof jar sits inside the wood cutout. The hinged door is held in place by a magnet and washer.

141

Use a new or sharpened ½-inch chisel. If you have not worked with a wood chisel before, then go slowly and read up on woodworking safety. You never want that chisel to be pointing towards you or one of your fingers. The other trick is to take out only small chunks with each pass.

Use a hammer to start at one corner of the outline. Bang it in about 1/8-inch all around the outline. Next place the chisel at one end and about 30-degrees and start to core out the center. Go slowly and carefully. A sharp chisel will cut out about 1/8-inch at a time with each pass. Time yourself as you go down into the wood in 1/8-inch steps. It's right about now that you may decide on using a much smaller container for your cache! The goal is to cut out a cylindrical bowl shape into each side.

If you're a neat freak, you can also buy a rounded, U-shaped chisel to make a nice smooth finish to the cut-out. You may also want to sand away the burs and splinters.

You will need to cut out both halves of the log. Once the cutout is big enough to hold your container, attach the two halves back again with metal hinges. Be sure to the edges line up nicely, so that when the flap is closed it looks like a solid log. You may need to spray paint the exposed cut edges to darken them to the bark color.

For my project I drilled a half-inch hole on one side and glued in a rare rare-earth magnet of the same size. On the facing surface I screwed in a metal washer as a contact plate for the magnet. This keeps the door closed, protecting the hide.

If you're like me, the two halves will not quite line up properly. Don't worry. This will be hidden in the woods with other branches and debris, and a man going by on horseback will never notice the minor flaws. If it's really bad, reinstall the hinges or use a lot of black spray paint to cover up the flaws. The whole idea is to make it fun for other geocachers, not necessarily to showcase your carpentry skills.

12. Birdhouse Conversion

A birdhouse makes a great hiding spot, as the container is already available, and most passers-by will think it's simply a birdhouse. Modifications are needed so one side opens like a door and a more waterproof container can be stored there.

Birdhouses are like key chains: they are everywhere and a dime a dozen. Be sure to check your local discount centers. You can build a simple birdhouse yourself, but it can be difficult and time consuming, so I favor buying a well worn one in a thrift store. Try to find one where one wall will come out easily so you can make a hinged door to hide a cache inside.

In the example shown here there is no easy way to take out one wall without the whole structure collapsing, so an easy solution is to use a box saw to cut away one section of the back. Then you can pry the panel off and make a hinged door out of it as shown, **Figure A-13**.

Figure A-13. A back panel is sawed open and pried off.

145

Use a punch to start the screw holes so it lines up properly. You may want to add some spray paint for protection to the exposed raw wood.

I also added a magnet inside mounted on a simple elbow bracket, **Figure A-14**. The magnet attracts a washer glued onto the door flap to keep it closed. There is still plenty of room to fit a 6-ounce plastic container inside. I like this arrangement because you have an outer disguise, an inner waterproof container, and if you're a worry-wort you can also enclose the log in a plastic bag. That provides three levels of protection.

Be sure to add a piece of screening to the bird entrance or some kind of barrier to keep them out.

Figure A-14. Use a punch to mark the hinge screw locations so that the door flap aligns properly. You can add a magnet inside and a metal washer so it stays shut in the wind. There is still room for the inner jar.

147

13. False Utility Box

Utility boxes, control panels, and wiring enclosures are visible everywhere in urban environments. They might be electrical junction boxes, water sprinkler controls, or telephone wiring panels. They all broadcast the same unspoken message: "Don't Touch!" And that's exactly why they make good hiding places for caches. A passer-by would never guess it's a geocaching container.

Real utility boxes often have electric wires inside and therefore they are sealed with screws or locks to keep the public out. In order to make the box look real, yet allow geocachers to open it without a screwdriver, we will need to add a hinge so that the front (or rear) panel opens easily. Then we will need to add a magnetic latch to hold it in place. **Figure A-15** shows a utility box spray painted a dark color and mounted to a fence post. You'll notice the edges of the box have built-in connecting flanges, so you can screw it right onto any wooden surface. The screw on the front panel give the suggestion that the box is sealed shut, but it actually flips up and you can put a waterproof container inside. In the upper right section of this photo you can see the bathroom cabinet style magnet that keeps the door closed as it lines up with the two glued-on metal washers in the flipped up cover plate.

Adding the hinge and magnet can be cumbersome for someone not used to working with shop tools. The utility box itself can be made of metal or plastic. The plastic ones are easier to drill for adding the hinge, but they can crack too. The metal ones are sturdier, but harder to drill.

Both plastic and metal utility boxes are not very waterproof. They have coin-shaped punch-out holes designed to make it easy for the electrician to add pipes that contain the wires for the box. These pipes are connected to the box with standard slip-ring tubular hardware (lower photo, right) that connects the pipe to the utility box. That lower photo shows other types of utility boxes, both a plastic and a metal version.

These utility boxes are made to connect to metal conduit tubing, but simple PVC pipe is much cheaper and easier to work with. I often connect the PVC pipe to an elbow that makes it appear as if it's going into the wall or the wooden support, but it's actually just glued in place.

Materials List

- 1 wooden board or fence plank to mount the box.

- 1 electric utility box.

- ½-inch PVC pipe, about 6 inches long.

- 1 PVC ½-inch elbow.

- One slip-ring cylinder to connect the PVC pipe to the punch-out hole.

- 1 cabinet magnet holder, or refrigerator magnets that you can glue in place.

- Gorilla glue.

- 1 cabinet door hinge with connecting hardware.

- Electric drill for hinge mounting.

- Optional: Spray paint for camouflage; cabinet knob to help open the faceplate door.

Practical matters

Start by paying a visit to the electricians section of the hardware store, and take a look at the various shapes and sizes of the utility boxes you can use. Measure the inside space so you can choose a jar or container that will fit inside and provide better waterproofing.

You'll need to decide where and how the box will be positioned. If there is no wooden surface you can attach it to, you may have to pound a section of PVC piping into the ground like a tent stake and simply mount the box on that.

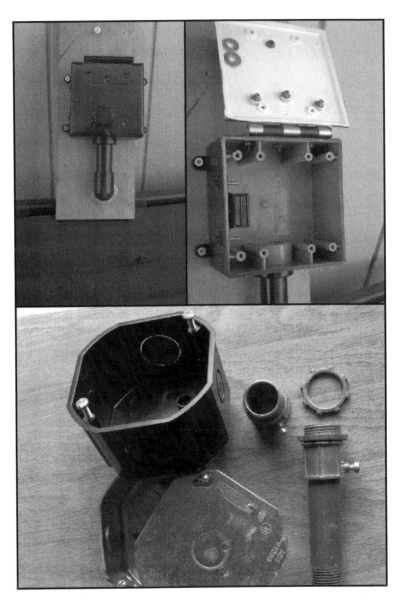

Figure A-15. Utility electrical boxes blend in well.

The boxes have several "punch-out" holes. You will need to punch out one of these where the external pipe will be connected.

Look at cabinet hinges while you are at the hardware store. You will have to pick the size of the hinge to match a clear mounting side on the utility box. The cover plate to the box has screw connectors on the inside. You will need to snip off the screws and glue the heads into place. Then on the inside you'll see the sockets for the screws. These should be snipped about 1/8th inch too, and with any luck you can mount a small magnet there to hold the cover plate closed.

14. Magnetically Sealed Enclosure

The basic concept here is to use magnets to hold together the parts of an object that normally don't come apart. A 4x4-inch fence post, for example, is always perceived as a solid structure. This project uses two pieces of U-shaped wood pieces that are connected by magnets and when placed together they look just like a solid piece of wood. Of course you can use the same idea for metal panels, control boxes, or even a false branch on a tree.

The hardest part of this project is gathering all the supplies. You can probably find everything you need at the hardware store, but I often like to buy some items on line, so I can get a bulk discount. The wood I selected is a grooved timber used in fencing; these are readily available in most lumber yards. If you can find a variation on this type of pre-formatted wood, you might be able to find something with a larger interior cavity, so that you can hide a something larger than the bison tube shown here.

The magnets are best bought on line, if you have the patience to wait for delivery. Even a huge hardware store won't always have the fantastic variety of magnets you can find on the Internet. The Internet, meanwhile, has every conceivable size and shape, and you can buy several at a time.

There are four different types of magnets, but the most popular are the black ferrite magnets that you find in refrigerator magnets, and the more powerful Neodymium Iron Boron (NIB) magnets, commonly referred to as rare earth magnets. Both come in standard sizes, such as half-inch and 3/4-inch disks. **Figure A-16**, top, shows three different disk magnets: a solid half-inch NIB disk, a half-inch NIB with a countersunk screw hole (on top of the drill bit), and a ¾-inch black ferrite disk on top of the ¾-inch drill bit.

A small 1/8th inch thick black ferrite magnet will cost between 10-cents and 15-cents when bought in bulk. A half-inch wide, 1/8th-inch thick NIB magnet will cost between 50-cents and 60-cents in bulk. Those with a hole drilled in the middle are near a dollar each, but the hole allows you to simply screw the magnet in place and avoid messy glues. Be careful with the NIB magnets: they are powerful enough to pinch a finger.

The easiest way to create a wooden enclosure with magnets is to drill a hole in the wood and use a mallet to pound the same sized magnet into the hole. For the opposite side on the facing plate, you can place either another magnet to match the first, or a simple metal disk that is attracted to the magnet.

Matching the two halves of the wood to each other is MUCH more difficult than it seems. This is due to three confounding influences.

- The magnets in each half (or the magnet and the attracting plate) have to match up exactly, or else the two halves don't sit right and this exaggerates the seam. Be sure to measure the center point on both halves exactly, then use a tiny drill (1/16th-inch) for a starter hole for the larger wood bit.

- You have to drill the wood hole pretty close to the actual thickness of the magnet. If it sinks in too far it may not attract the opposite side. If it's too shallow, the magnet will not be flush with the wood surface. Practice with the drill on a spare piece of wood in order to get the correct depth. If you drill down too far, partially fill in the hole with some glue and sawdust to raise the level.

- Even with a tight fit the magnet can come out of the hole, so you need to glue it in place. Glues and wood putty work OK, but they are quite messy. Consider buying the more expensive magnets with the countersunk screw hole in the center.

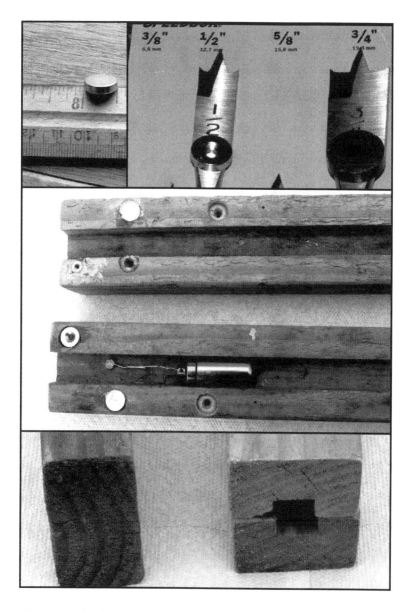

Figure A-16. Magnets seal the container. Drill bits match the magnet sizes.

157

The photos I've enclosed show an early version of this project, with all the messy adhesives, misplaced holes, and sloppy craftsmanship, **Figure A-16**, center. Despite all the errors it can still work decently, but you should at least *try* to make it look professional.

In mounting the enclosure in the field you may want to add a piece to the top to cover the hole, **Figure A-16**, bottom, or attach a mounting stake to the enclosure so you can simply nail it in place onto a fence post.

Obviously, you can use the same magnet technique to clamp two parts of anything together in order to make a well camouflaged container. Magnets work well with plastic and metal containers although mounting the magnets on wood and metal takes more skill.

15. Sheet Metal Cache Wrap

A cache wrap is a cheap and easy way to camouflage a container by recycling sheet metal art or decorations and wrapping them around the cache. Most thrift shops have copper plate, brass, tin or other metals that can be molded around a cache with a rubber mallet.

This may be hard to explain, but when you see it you'll know it. Walk into any thrift store and you'll see these discarded, semi-antique wall and garden decorations that have seen better days. It may be an artistic tin-sheet fish or a cheap metal garden frog, but one look at it and you can see that with a snip here and some banging there you could cover that otherwise drab mayonnaise jar that you call a cache.

Many of these pieces are thin sheet metal supported by heavier gauge wiring. You may have to anchor the artwork onto your container using hardware or lots of duct tape, but it works. The best bet is to show some cxamples, **Figure A-17**.

Figure A-17. Tin and sheet metal floral decorations are used as wraps around a cache.

Once you find copper, sheet metal, or heavy foil materials, you can match them up with standard containers and use a rubber mallet to pound them into shape around the container, **Figure A-18**. The matching to the inner container does not have to be perfect, but it should provide enough cover to obscure the view of the container, and it should be attached somehow. Zip ties, tape, and clue all work fairly well.

The advantage of this technique is that it can be used to provide a cover or mask for otherwise hard to conceal objects.

Figure A-18. Bronze, copper and sheet metal can be used as a mask.

Other books by Vince Migliore

Creative Cache Containers for Geocaching, ISBN-13 # 978-1477635711, June 2012: Superseded by this book.

Metal Detecting for the Beginner, ISBN-13 # 978-1452862453, March 2009.

The Art and Science of Metal Detecting, ISBN-13 # 978-1517225104, September, 2015.

A Measure of Heaven, Near-Death Experience Data Analysis, ISBN-11448611202, October, 2009.

Index

NOTES:

Made in the USA
San Bernardino, CA
18 July 2017